Up There to Step

Up There to Step

⚜

Play

Peddar Panga

© 2016 Peddar Panga
All rights reserved.

ISBN: 0692713158
ISBN 13: 9780692713150
Library of Congress Control Number: 2016907682
Peddar Panga, San Antonio, TX

To Augustin Mubiayi Mamba

Characters

———◆———

1) Arleta Yavanov, *seventy-year-old lad*
2) Arketta Yavanov, *daughter of Arleta. She is fifty-four years old.*
3) David Schumerman Jr., *seventeen-year-old boy.*
4) David Schumerman Sr., *father of David Jr. and Linzi's common-law husband.*
5) Linzi Longfen, *mother of David Jr.*
6) Lynnette Zibo, *David Jr.'s girlfriend (African American).*
7) Kassandra De Zavada, *older sister of David Jr.*
8) Jevus De Zadava, *a Hispanic guy with a great Spanish accent, husband of Kassandra.*
9) Belgina Kyaleza, *daughter of Arketta Yavanov, thirty-five years old.*
10) Kish Kyaleza, *a forty-year-old African American guy, husband of Belgina.*
11) Antonio Moretti, *a Christian clergyman from Italy. He has an Italian accent.*
12) Andricoco Longfen, *a police officer and Linzi's brother.*
13) Apolosa Shingoski, *Arketta's servant.*
14) Kapoza Sandrock, *Arketta's servant, lawyer, and personal financier.*
15) Kalol Adelita, *Arleta's female servant.*
16) Betsy, *a pregnant woman.*
17) Iberkonta Denis, *best friend of David Sr.*
18) Peta Lubang, *bartender at the airport and a makeup artist.*
19) Bunikenike, *an entity wearing a white dress.*
20) Three Hell entities.

Settings

---✦---

THE PLAY IS *set in 2024, in the fictive city of Aerosanam, fictive state of Jefferson, in the United States. The play has multiple scenes with different settings. Act 1, scene 1 is in an airport terminal. However, almost every scene takes place on a different set.*

For Act 1, scene 1, Upstage, going from Stage Left to Stage Right is a baggage claim booth, with the inscription "Aerosanam Airways Baggage Claim." Past the baggage claim booth is an airline service counter, then a long bench. A bar counter follows. It is set with two elevated stools for customers. Away from the bar counter, still going from Stage Left to Stage Right, is a door with the inscription "Ladies." It is the ladies' restroom. A barricade is seen in Upstage Right. It is the police checkpoint and a gateway for all passengers toward the boarding gates. A wall, or just a curtain, is seen in the Right Wing. An entrance gate for arriving passengers is seen down the wing.

Act One

SCENE I

Aerosanam International Airport. Lights come up and reveal a busy airport terminal. People with carry-on bags are walking back and forth. Other passengers are being searched at the security checkpoint, where Andricoco, a police officer with the Aerosanam Police Department, is conducting the airport standard security searches. David Sr., David Jr., Kassandra, and Linzi are sitting on the bench. David Sr. is reading a newspaper. Linzi is sleeping on his shoulder. Kassandra is leaning on her mother's shoulder, sleeping. David Jr. is sleeping with one hand on one arm of the bench. At the bar, the bartender, Peta, is serving liquor shots to Kish and Kalol. The two are engaged in a conversation, so far limited to gestures. They stop for couple seconds and pay a listening ear to the announcements from the airport speakers.

SPEAKERS [*A female voice announces*]. Welcome to the Aerosanam International Airport. The weather is so very lovely today. The sky is clear, with scattered clouds. The current temperature at the airport is twenty degrees Celsius. We have only a five percent chance of rain. So enjoy your flights."

After couple seconds, another female voice announces on the speakers.

SPEAKERS. Mr. Kapoza Sandrock is asked to report to gate six to board Aerosanam Airways flight QC seven-eighty-seven."

Kapoza enters the stage walking very fast toward the checkpoint, pulling his carry-on bag. At his side is Apolosa, his friend. When Kapoza gets to the check-point, Apolosa stops. Kapoza is searched then. Kish, who has been drinking and gesturing with Kalol, sees Apolosa. He comes and greets him.

KISH [*Smiling broadly*]. Eh, buddy, long time!
APOLOSA [*Smiling broadly, too*]. Yeah, long time. [*They shake hands and hug.*] You don't stop at your grandma's anymore. What's wrong?
KISH. Da's why I'm here, at the airport. My wife's been gone for four months on a cruise vacation ta da Bahamas. She took her flight back, earlier today, from Key West, Florida. [*He looks at his watch.*] She be landing soon. You know, I can't come visit her grandma by myself.
APOLOSA. I gotcha. [*He points at Kapoza.*] You probably don't know my friend, Kapoza, right? [*Kish shakes his head.*] He's a lawyer and the new Mafioso of your mother-in-law. She fired Adisi, who proved to be less

3

efficient than she expected. You know Adisi, right? [*Kish nods.*] He's gone. He gave all his entire life to the service of Arketta. However, she forgot all his good fighting spirit for just a little mistake he made. It looks as if a single mistake is worth more than millions of good deeds. Now the boss asked me to find a replacement for Adisi, and then I brought Kapoza. [*Kapoza has just passed the checkpoint (putting on the belt and shoes that he took off for the search) and disappears through the gate.*]

KISH. [*Pointing at Kalol.*] Da's my cousin, Kalol. She be workin' with ya guys there.

APOLOSA. [*Delighted.*] Ah! I've heard that Megan Mwakuj, the girl with larger hips like an airport tarmac, did quit yesterday. I was off yesterday. I think your cousin'll be her replacement.

KISH. Exactly. I took her here to welcome my wife, an' tomorrow she starts her shift at yo boss's place.

APOLOSA. Tell her welcome to our world, man. Just advise her that it ain't like everywhere else. We live in a different world, at the mercy of the Great Arketta.

KISH. Arleta.

APOLOSA. No. Not Arleta but Arketta. It's actually your mother-in-law, Arketta, who runs the vibrations around your grandmother-in-law's bungalow. We like it anyway.

KISH. Man! There're two categories of slaves: field slave an' home slave. If y'ask a field slave ta run away, he do so without knowin' why he runnin' an' in which direction he goin'. In contrast, if y'ask a home slave ta run away, he may even kill ya. He won't abide leaving da fake comfort he believes he's enjoyin'. A home slave knows dat he's a damn slave, but he likes it.

APOLOSA. I'm neither of them. Slavery is something from the past. Let's regret it through history only. It ain't a headline subject anymore.

KISH. Well, I was just sayin'. [*Changing the subject.*] Where's yo friend goin'?

APOLOSA. Kapoza?

KISH. Yeah!

APOLOSA. I don't know. Your mother-in-law gave me an order to drop him at the airport. I can't ask where he's going.

KISH. He couldn't tell ya?

APOLOSA. I din't ask. I wish he could go for a long while.

KISH. Why's dat?

APOLOSA. I bang his wife.

KISH. What?

APOLOSA. It ain't my faults. It's his wife herself who's always behind me, following me like a dog. I guess she gotta be highly contented that her husband's gone today.

KISH. You're mordant, Apolosa. I'm scared of ya a'ready.

APOLOSA. I ain't dangerous. It's kind of a fatality. Life has its manner of packing things that're less understood by humankind.

KISH. You bang yo friend's wife. Then you reward him with a highly lucrative job, right? [*They laugh heartily.*]

APOLOSA. Life may send you to walk barefoot over country roads full of thorns. It hurts, but you find curiously that you like it and you lack power to overcome it.

KISH. I'm wondering, what pushes some women to look for extramarital affairs?

APOLOSA. I don't know. Maybe they're unsatisfied by their husband's performance, or maybe 'cause they're just whores.

KISH. Now I'm scared dat my wife was gone fer four long months. She probably needed her stuff scratched in.

APOLOSA. Who knows? If I were you, I'd never let my wife go without me for so many months.

KISH. I trust her, anyway.

APOLOSA. That's the magic word: trust. However, trust ain't a blank check where you can write anything. [*Kish shakes his head.*] Women are so intelligent. Women know to keep a secret, like a dead buried body.

KISH. We ain't able ta live without women, though.

APOLOSA. Good luck, man! I hope your wife kept it just for yourself. After four months, she'll be like a virgin again. Enjoy it, man!

KISH. You enjoy it with yo mistress! She probably waitin' for ya, with her roots wide open.

APOLOSA. Man, I gotta go.

KISH. All right, man! You probably gonna see me soon at yo boss's place, man. Y' know, my wife'll be here soon.

They shake hands and hug. Apolosa walks away toward the exit. On his way out, Betsy, a pregnant beggar woman stops him. She stands very close to him, her belly touching him. She makes hands gestures that tells Apolosa that she wants something to eat. He gives her a couple bills from his wallet and they both exist. Kish returns to the bar, where Kalol is now standing with a glass in her hand, facing the audience. Peta, the bartender, is arranging bottles and wiping the bar.

KALOL. Why do men always lie?

KISH. Women's ears were especially made to hear lies only. If ya tell 'em da truth, they won't buy nor believe it. But with lies, they believe 'em faster, quicker, an' easier. Is dat make sense?

KALOL. Was the tongue of a man made specially for lying? If it says the truth, it sounds like lies, and truth doesn't click. Only lies sound credible from a male's mouth. Check yo own beliefs.

KISH. [*To Peta.*] Hey, lovely! Can ya serve us two more shots, please?

PETA. Sure! Do you want it neat or straight up?

KISH. Just add some ice cubes an' a twisted lemon, please.

PETA. All right, sir!

KALOL. [*To Kish.*] I ain't convinced. Why do men usually lie to women?

KISH. Truth hurts. A woman is a soft creature who needs to be spoken to easily an' softly. Tellin' her da truth will damage her the most.

Peta mixes the drinks and serves two glasses of liquor. She hands one to Kish first, who politely refuses it.

KISH. Oh Peta. Do ya wanna break the local rules, or what?
PETA. What do you mean by "local rules"?
KISH. Ladies first, please!

Peta smiles and hands the glass of liquor to Kalol.

PETA. Is that "ladies first" rule applicable everywhere?
KISH. Maybe, maybe not. I never heard any restriction to it. [*He is drunk and starting to lose control over his tongue.*] I'm black, strong, and more capable than a white man.
PETA. Why you bringin' in an off subject? We not speakin' of white men.
KISH. White men believe that they're capable of everything. They believe they're in control of this world. The truth is that they're less strong than blacks.
PETA. I'm lost, and I can't understand you. A' you complexed about whites?
KISH. They're complexed 'bout blacks. 'Cause we're stronger than 'em.
PETA. 'Cause your ancestors made crops for them, you believe that whites weren't physically strong enough to plow the land? [*She returns to her business, leaving Kish and Kalol to talk.*]
KISH. To be strong is to have more than one woman. How can white men claim to be strong when they're unable to have more than one woman? To have one woman's like to have one eye only.
KALOL. Do you have two women?
KISH. I din't say that. I said that I'm able like Solomon to have more than one woman. Solomon in the Christian Bible's reported to have married one thousand women.
KALOL. Solomon was black?
KISH. Semites are blacks.
KALOL. [*She chuckles.*] I never heard you before with such jokes.
KISH. I'm serious.
KALOL. Solomon was possessed by a spirit of prostitution. The dog spirit.

KISH. No. He's believed by all to be the greatest wise man of all times.

KALOL. Where's wisdom about changing wives like underwear? To taste their bodies' recipes?

KISH. Maybe! Women taste differently.

KALOL. So what? [*She looks around.*] Solomon is quoted saying that all is vanity. So where's that benefit of tasting different women's legs?

KISH. I wish he was around an' you could ask him in person.

KALOL. You said you were following his lead.

KISH. Solomon was strong. That's it. He was able to handle more dan a thousand women. He was really strong. Women are like wild elephants, heavy an' slow to move around. But movin' a herd of thousand elephants? He was strong and wise. Otherwise he could be crushed down.

KALOL. Whoever has one woman is weak?

KISH. Arguably, yes.

KALOL. If you serious, you need to know that we live in a society where we're called to interact and support each other. Nobody's capable of every-thing. Strong and weak are called to help each other interdependently. It's nothin' to do with race or gender.

Peta continues to do her chores at the bar. Kalol drinks a shot, frowns, and then puts her glass on the counter.

KALOL. Hammer out the difficulties!

KISH. Can't you drink without frownin' yo face?

KALOL. You been elongating your lips with every shot. Can't you over-come that?

KISH. [*To Peta.*] Two more shots, please.

Peta mixes the drinks and hands the first glass to Kalol. Kish reaches to take it. Peta avoids Kish's hand and holds the glass.

PETA. Ladies first!

KISH. What?

KALOL. She said ladies first.
KISH. I can put my skirt on.
KALOL. That won't make you a lady.
KISH. At least it may help me to be put on the top of any list. It has worked for others. Remember Jamie Foxx?
KALOL. You're drunk.
KISH. I'm not.
KALOL. A drunk person, a snoozing person, and a thief are alike. They never admit their fault.

Peta gives a glass of liquor first to Kalol and then to Kish.

KISH. The rule should be "black first."
PETA. [*Laughing.*] Jesus! Why is that?
KISH. 'Cause I'm black. I'm gonna write that rule on every face of all colored men living in Aerosanam.
KALOL. You are drunk.
PETA [*To Kish*]. Are you black?
KISH. What do you mean by dat? Am I undercolored?
PETA. You're black? I didn't know you were a black man. I ain't joking, but I've seen many black men around. They got nothing in common with you.
KISH. Only 'cause I married up? Is that 'cause my wife is a billionaire?
PETA. No really! You are—[*Peta's cell phone rings. She shows her index finger to Kish.*] Hold on, please! [*She answers her cell phone.*] Hallo? [*She walks away.*]

Kassandra, who was sitting on the waiting bench with her family, stands up and walks in the direction of the bathroom. Jevus, Kassandra's husband, enters the scene just before Kassandra stood up. Kassandra passes in front of Kish and Kalol. Kish slaps Kassandra's butt. Kalol smiles and shakes her head. Kassandra continues to walk without turning around. She just wipes with her hand the part of her butt that was slapped.

Jevus witnesses how Kish touched his wife's butt. He stands still for a while.

KALOL. Typical men! I usually wonder why men are so obsessed by females' butts. Can you tell me why?

KISH. I believe it's 'cause the butt is where da beauty of a woman lays.

Kish tries to drink another shot, but Kalol blocks him. She holds his glass.

KALOL. [*Smiling.*] I can't 'low you to drink anymore.

KISH. Because?

KALOL. I don't 'low myself to be dominated by anything, including alcohol. I don't 'low those around me to be dominated by alcohol either.

KISH. 'Cause you got Russian roots? Russians a' so arrogant. They think they control alcohol. They think they can't get drunk. They think—

KALOL. You getting drunk!

KISH. Me? Hell no.

KALOL. I know you can't admit it.

KISH. Of course, I can't admit to be drunk when I ain't.

KALOL. A drunkard is like a thief. They both don't admit their wrongdoing. A thief won't admit that he stole. So is a drunkard. He can't admit that he's drunk.

KISH. [*He points at his chest.*] Kish Kyaleza has his own testing technique to know if he's drunk or not. Do you wanna know?

KALOL. [*Nodding.*] Rise one foot up to see if you still in balance?

KISH. Not really. I spit up. If my spit doesn't go far, an' my saliva falls on my chest, then I can conclude dat I'm drunk.

Jevus starts walking toward the bar.

KALOL. Why you slapped that lady's butt then?

KISH. It was bubbling. She really walked too close to me, as if she was indirectly inviting me to spank it.

KALOL. Under normal circumstances, do you think you could slap an unknown woman's butt?

KISH. She enjoyed it. Women like to be spanked on their butt. See? She didn't even react. She wanted more slaps.
KALOL. You are drunk.

Jevus approaches slowly to the bar counter, and he grabs Kish's shirt by the collar with his left hand and prepares to punch him with his right hand.

JEVUS. [*Confident and very calm.*] Jou spanked my woman's butt.
KISH. [*Surprised.*] What? Me?
JEVUS. I saw jou. Jou touched my wife's butt.
KISH. She got no butt. She has no butt at all. I just suggested she puts some Styrofoam in her underwear to pop her behind up.

Kalol tries to intervene, but Jevus pushes her. She screams and falls down on her butt. After couple seconds, she stands up, intimidated, and runs away toward the exit.

JEVUS. Flat or not, jou invaded a private space dat belongs exclusively to me.
KISH. But I didn't take it with me.
JEVUS. I own dat butt. Jou cannot touch it and walk easily away, unpunished.
KISH. What? Do ya own yo wife? [*He laughs.*] That's the funniest thing I've ever heard in my entire life. I'll tell dat to my wife when she gets back.
JEVUS. I will make jour *culo* play music.
KISH. Da's what I call shit.

Jevus clenches his fist, ready to strike.

KISH. [*Using his hands in sign of stop.*] Eh eh eh, don't. [*Jevus stops and looks at him steadily.*] One last request before ya hit me. [*Jevus nods.*] Did you say she's yo woman?

JEVUS. She is my woman. Why did you touch my woman's *culo?*
KISH. She has no butt. Take a look at her behind; it's flat like a wall. How can I touch something dat doesn't even exist?

Jevus clenches and draws back his fist to hit Kish.

KISH. [*He makes hands gestures again to make him stop.*] Ehhhhh, stop! [*Jevus stops.*] Before ya hit me, lemme make sure that I understood ya better. Lemme ask you again. Did ya say dat she's yo woman?
JEVUS. Of course she is.
KISH. How can she be yo woman when ya met her in a bar and ya claim that she's yo woman?
JEVUS. Who told jou that I found her in a bar?
KISH. I'm just guessing, but it's damn true, right?
JEVUS. Jes.
KISH. How come she bought you cartoon DVDs, and she leaves ya at home watchin' cartoons while she goes out to party nightly in bars?
JEVUS. How did jou know dat?
KISH. I'll tell you only after you release yo grab on me.
JEVUS. Okay! I will release my grab, *pero* under one condition. Only if jou agree to tell me how jou know what you just told me. [*Kish nods.*]

Belgina enters the scene from the entrance gate for arriving passengers, pulling a carry-on bag. She sees Jevus grabbing her husband. She walks in their direction.
    Jevus releases his grab on Kish's collar. Kish runs away toward the left wing. He didn't see Belgina. Jevus stays still.

KISH. [*Running.*] She ain't yo woman. [*He stops when he is a safe distance away.*] She tells everybody yo story. How you act like a little kid an' how she locks ya out if you get back late at night, but she goes out every day an' comes back home anytime she wants. In addition, ya have to open the door for her. That's what ya call yo woman? You got da courage to fight fer her?

Jevus moves as if he is about to chase Kish, then stops. Kish runs away and exits the scene. Jevus stays akimbo for couple of seconds. He shakes his head and punches one fist into the other hand. As soon as he turns around, Belgina grabs him by his collar. At first, Jevus is startled, then he stays still.

BELGINA. [*She's holding her carry-on bag in her left hand on and has her right on Jevus's collar.*] I saw you abusing and intimidating my husband. You can't walk away like that. There're great consequences for yo' crime.
JEVUS. [...] Heh!
BELGINA. See how you look like a stupid snake. You just ruined my so-dreamed homecoming moment. My husband told me that he created a great surprise for me. You spoiled my day. You got hell to pay.
JEVUS. Now jou just getting dead wrong. Do jou feel de force behind those words?
BELGINA. I can tell that you not from here, are you? [*She grabs harder.*] Are you from Aerosanam?
JEVUS. Do not be upset with me.
BELGINA. Boy, you're committing one of the oldest sins, rebellion. Lucifer was the first to raise against the almighty God. I wonder why you keep opening your mouth against me. Do you know who I am? I can make you sleep on top of a ten-ounces flying bird.

Kassandra enters the scene from the restroom. She explodes as she approaches her husband. David Jr. and Linzi, who were still sleeping on the bench, have just woken up and approach Kassandra from behind, trying to calm her and pull her away from the quarrel. David Sr. doesn't move. He continues to read his newspaper as if nothing were happening.

KASSANDRA. [*Screaming.*] Jevus! Is that one of your babies' mama? [*She looks at Belgina.*] She's even older than you are.
JEVUS. I do not know her.
KASSANDRA. [*Screaming. David Jr. is holding her.*] You don't know her? You think you can fool me every time? Why is she grabbing you on your collar?

JEVUS. Ask her! She is showin' revenge for her husband.
KASSANDRA. Who is her husband? What did you do to her husband?
JEVUS. Just ask her. She is well positioned to answer jour questions.
KASSANDRA. Why then you made kids with so many women?
JEVUS. First, dis is not my woman. Second, in de US, kids are a liability. Where I am from, children are wealth.

Andricoco, the police officer, approaches the group. David Jr. and Linzi pull Kassandra away to the bench. They sit her down, still holding her. Andricoco handcuffs Jevus.

JEVUS. Be careful with those handcuffs. I have a pacemaker installed on my chest. Jou may shock me.

Andricoco drags Jevus away from Belgina. They stop in front of the baggage claim booth. Belgina dials her phone and talks with gestures.

ANDRICOCO. What are you doing, fella?
JEVUS. *Fui un senior negro que pago el culo de mi esposa. Yo soy un caballero—*
ANDRICOCO. I don't speak a word of Spanish!
JEVUS. *Yo ti entendí hablando Español el otra día na casa de su hermaná.*
ANDRICOCO [*Raising his voice.*] I don't speak any Spanish at all!
JEVUS. Uncle, listen to me—
ANDRICOCO. I don't need to listen to you. You need to be careful in this city. There're people that are untouchable in Aerosanam.
JEVUS. Jou should have pressed charges against de black dude instead of arresting me. Dere was an offense caught on cameras of dis airport. A sexual abuse case. It is a redhead felony.
ANDRICOCO. I don't know what you talking about. I saw you attempting to fight an untouchable person.
JEVUS. I did not do anyteeng. Earlier, there was a black guy who touched my wife's butt.

ANDRICOCO. Was it why Belgina grabbed your collar?

JEVUS. Jou know dat lady by her name?

ANDRICOCO. She's the granddaughter of the almighty Arleta.

JEVUS. Arleta, de multibijionaire lady?

ANDRICOCO. Of course! There's no vocabulary to describe the power that Arleta possesses in this town. Everybody bows when facing that lady. So if you wanna stay alive, be a man enough to avoid trouble with anybody in Arleta's circle. The black guy you talkin' about married up. He's Belgina's husband.

JEVUS. Well, I apologize. I did not know all dis. Are jou going to press charges?

ANDRICOCO. I forgive you for now. Only because I'm related to your mother-in-law. On the other hand, don't forget my advice: stay away from Arleta's circle.

JEVUS. Okay, Uncle!

ANDRICOCO. Moreover, don't take advantage of my good nature and 'cause I'm related to your mother-in-law. I'm afraid that you'll do it again. It's a voice coming from my experience.

JEVUS. If jou drink beer, it means that jou are supposed to get addicted?

ANDRICOCO. [*Opening the handcuffs on Jevus.*] Yes! You just inviting the addiction trait into your life. Chinese will tell you that a thousand miles' trip always starts with one step.

Kish and Kalol enters. She is holding a bouquet of flowers.
  Andricoco releases the handcuffs from Jevus's hands.
  Jevus perceives Kish entering.

JEVUS. [*He points at Kish.*] Dat's him. [*He tries to charge his body to attack Kish.*] He touched my wife's butt.

Kish sees Jevus move and minimize it. He throw a hand in his direction, not intimidated at all.

15

ANDRICOCO. [*He holds Jevus by the hand.*] If you move again, [*he shows Jevus the handcuffs*] I'll charge you for disturbing the peace and for encroaching on airport security. Trust me: you'll spend years in prison.

JEVUS. [*Recoiling.*] My bad. *Pero* I have a question, please.

ANDRICOCO. As long as your question can spare you a variety of consequences, go ahead.

JEVUS. Does dat guy go around Aerosanam touching women's butts?

ANDRICOCO. Do me a favor that can save your butt: act as if you don't have a tongue. Actually, you didn't see anything. That'll keep you out of trouble in Aerosanam. It goes without saying that the guy you touched is untouchable and very powerful.

JEVUS. If he is powerful and untouchable, is he supposed to be abusing his power? He is a bully, and jou guys, law enforcement, are afraid of him.

ANDRICOCO. Justice doesn't mean that you want law enforcement to do it your way. Keep your head in the sand. May be better in the water. Here, things are different. Go kiss anybody's ass if that's gonna help you calm down.

JEVUS. Where I am from, touching a married woman's butt doesn't happen. That is more dan an insult; it is a killing offense.

ANDRICOCO. Then go back to your country, or learn something different. Things happen differently in this city of Aerosanam. You can't breathlessly try to parallel-park countries.

Kish has walked past Andricoco and Jevus. He gets to his wife and welcomes her. They hug, and he gives her flowers. Then, they exit. .

ANDRICOCO. You are violating the security code of this airport. But I'll let you go. Today is your lucky day.

JEVUS. I am just a little ant. How can an ant break de security code?

ANDRICOCO. In matters of security, we do not underestimate even a little ant. It can cause tremendous damage. Anyway, today is your lucky day. You are free to go.

Up There to Step

Andricoco returns to the checkpoint. Jevus walks to the bench, where his wife and her family are sitting.

KASSANDRA. [*Standing up.*] You see how your eyes are reddened for always trying to sniff under women's skirts? You usually play with women, don't you? You see how you found a true woman champion who put you on a commode of a Middle Age bathroom. I believe they didn't have same accommodations in the bathrooms during the Middle-Age as we do have today, did they? What was it that you defecated? Diarrhea or dysentery? Your eyes are so red that I thought you struggled a lot in the bathroom. You look really like the human-waste issue.

JEVUS. That woman *fui defendiendo a su esposo.* I would better praise a woman like her who stands for her husband first. *Pero* jou, jou are just making every effort to put me down. Jou are supposed to give the best of jourself to dis marriage. *Pero* jou have been giving de worst so far. It is not late, dough. Jou can still change.

KASSANDRA. You see now? [*Looking at her mother.*] Mom, did you hear what he just said? He's praising another woman than his wife. [*To Jevus.*] I'm supposed to be your best, no matter what.

JEVUS. I am supposed to be de best of all, not a human-waste issue to jou.

LINZI. Stop it guys! You not supposed to be quarreling in from of your parents and parents-in-law. More less, you can't be arguing in public. Any issue between you guys has to be handled in your bedroom.

Lynette Zibo, the invitee of the David family, arrives. She enters the scene from the passengers' arriving gate. Jevus points at her. Kassandra turns her head, sees her, and jumps.

KASSANDRA. [*Speaking with joy to her family.*] There she is!

The whole family stands up. Hugs and kisses follow, as Lynette is welcomed. After the excitement of the welcome, Linzi invites the family into a circle.

LINZI. [*To Lynnette.*] I'm glad that you made it. Our family will have to apologize to you extremely for all the hard times we gave you for the last two years you've been dating David. We never wanted and approved our David to date or to marry a colored girl. So we opposed your relationship, and in our power as parents, we did everything possible to impede it. But all our efforts were just making your relationship stronger. We ultimately decided to run away from you. We left New England and relocated here in Aerosanam, hoping to close your case forever. Unfortunately, just a week after our relocation, our family was hit by a nuclear weapon. Once in Aerosanam, we thought to have solved the problem of your relationship with David. But, another tragedy gigantically unbearable hit us. We failed to handle it on our own. We tried to go back to New England, but the woman we are fighting against seems in control of our family. Therefore, we decided to bring you here today. We want you to marry our son David as soon as possible.

Lynnette is pleased. She is smiling. David Jr. drops to one knee, takes Lynnette's left arm, and shows her a ring.

DAVID JR. All the stars' eyes are focused here. The moon and the sun are all joining us to witness the greatest proposal in the history of the humankind. The cells of my heart are vibrating. For the honor of all the galaxies assisting and witnessing, from millions of miles away, this big bang explosion between the heart of my rib, Lynnette and my own heart, and on behalf of my family present here, I would like to spend the rest of my life with you. [*Breath.*] Lynnette, would you marry me, please?
LYNNETTE. [*Joyfully, putting her hand around her mouth. Heartily smiling.*] Yes! Yes! Yes!

David Jr. puts the ring on Lynnette's finger. A wedding song plays, and David's family, except the David Sr. throw flower petals on the couple.
　　After the little ceremony, all the members of the family, except Kassandra, walk to the exit. Jevus is walking with the family. When he realizes that his wife

18

has stayed behind, he stops to wait for her. Kassandra dials her phone. Jevus hears her phone conversation.

KASSANDRA. [*Speaking on the phone.*] The code's D-L-W-oh-seven by tomorrow...Okay...Thanks.

Kassandra finishes talking and joins her husband, and they walk to the exit.

Curtain.

SCENE 2
In David Schumerman Sr.'s living room.

DAVID SR. [*He finishes reading a text message on his cell phone. He shakes his head.*] It was Arketta. She says that what our family did at the airport should be considered as if it never happened.
LINZI. Who does she think she is?
DAVID JR. What makes her believe that it didn't happen?
DAVID SR. She added that David Jr. has to marry her mother whether he likes it or not.
LINZI. I ain't gonna accept it.
LYNNETTE. She lyin'.
LINZI. She knows all the mechanics of lying.
DAVID SR. She added that she's not joking, that whatever she says has to be executed, and that we don't have any other option.
LINZI. She's—
DAVID JR. This is not Facebook! It's not a social media network where everybody has to express his opinion the way he likes it. This is our lives that Arketta's trying to stick her finger inside. If we don't react, she'll remotely exercise her control over our lives because we believing in her words.
LINZI. My brother Andricoco warned me that she never jokes and that she's capable of anything.
DAVID JR. Only if we believe her. We gotta find a safe plan. The one we've tried, to bring Zibo to Aerosanam and have a proposal ceremony at airport, seems to haven't impressed her at all. She ain't gonna give up.
LYNNETTE. She may be just tranna scare us. We gotta just ignore her.
DAVID JR. Ignoring her may not work. We've tried that already. She still pressing hard. She keeps throwing fear vibrations all around.
LYNNETTE. There ain't no fear but only what you put in yo head. If you think she scarin' ya, so it gon be.
DAVID JR. Lynnette, we've heard that before. It doesn't apply practically when facing a real danger like Arketta. She's believed to be worse than the devil itself.

DAVID SR. Speaking of devil, I forgot to say my first lie.

LINZI. Your first lie?

DAVID SR. Arketta is left handed; that's why she acts like a devil. She's a *sinistra*.

LINZI. I don't understand you. That's a fact or a lie? I don't see any relevance to the subject at hand.

DAVID SR. From the ancient Greek, people believed that all left-handed people were evil. So they called them *sinistro*. [*He puts his index fingers up on either side of his head to simulate horns.*]

LYNNETTE. I heard that before.

DAVID SR. So I'm not making it up.

LYNNETTE. The right handed were called *dextro* an' were considered normal people.

LINZI. [*To David Sr.*] I don't see why you call it your first lie.

DAVID JR. Mom, Dad's joking.

LINZI. I don't see what jokes have to do with a serious life situation like this.

LYNNETTE. Dad ain't jokin'. He only sayin' that Arketta is evil an' should be regarded as so.

DAVID SR. Joke or not, here's how I see life. [*Sigh.*] The devil is real. He does everything in his might to make your life a living hell. It's your responsibility to gun him down.

DAVID JR. The devil is like a cartoon character. He dies and comes back to life every single time after you gun him down.

LYNNETTE. Why that Arketta is so obsessed with ma David only? If she the incarnation of the devil, she gotta give hard time to everybody not only to ma man. She believed by many to be generous.

DAVID SR. That's one of many unanswered questions. Her claim that God spoke to her mother about David Schumerman, doesn't stand up. It's just her nature, maybe. I did some research around the city, and there's no report that Arleta has been in a relationship with anybody for the last forty years.

DAVID JR. I believe that we need to avoid considering her as a devil. We giving her too much weight. The devil is more intelligent and cleverer than her. We need to just stop talking about the devil itself. It's a kind of unconscious invitation to the devil to dominate us. We need to deal with Arketta as a human being.

LINZI. That's easy to say. So far we've been turning around. Our decision should be to move up or to ward off Arketta's will.

LYNNETTE. Let's try to ignore her again.

DAVID JR. You have three choices: dance, and everybody gonna be laughing at you; sing, and you'll never come back from it; and choose nothing at all. Then you'll be officially declared a coward.

LYNNETTE. I ain't wanna go down the first two roads. But, if not doin' nothin' brings me victory; who cares even if people declare me a coward?

DAVID SR. Just put your sunglasses on when people declare you a coward.

DAVID JR. Speaking of sunglasses, I've heard crazy stories about Aerosanam. Every citizen of this city believe that Arketta's sunglasses are the same ones that Jesus wore in his time. They believe they possess tangible proof about their beliefs, only 'cause Arketta said it.

LINZI. Well! [*Deep breath.*] I'll never get tired of being impressed by the Aerosanam people and the Homo sapiens in general.

DAVID JR. That's curiously strange.

LINZI. Strange, indeed! That's why sometimes I like to talk to myself. I stand in front of the mirror, and I praise my accomplishments and discuss my projects and…

DAVID JR. [*At Lynnette, who's staring at him.*] You looking at me like you were in a dream.

DAVID SR. That's not a regular gaze. It's love in action. [*They all nod.*]

LYNNETTE. [*Smiling.*] Yeah, Dad's right! I love you, an' nobody gonna succeed in takin' ya away from me.

LINZI. [*Nodding.*] Nobody, indeed! And I'll make sure that nobody takes, my David, away from you. [*Big sigh.*] This whole situation is giving me the true wings of a woman. Never before have had I ever felt better about myself. I gotta fight.

DAVID SR [*To Linzi. He is rubbing the back of her neck.*] The entire family got your back.

LINZI. Thank you. I know that nobody is capable of everything. Even the one you think he loves you totally, will always have a deficiency somewhere. Even the Iron Lady Arketta, who's believed to be the strongest woman on earth, has her deficiencies. My mission is to find her weaknesses and strike her hard in them. [*Sigh.*] I promise: I'll make her feel like every other human being.

DAVID JR. You also need to relax, Mom. You displaying a whole lot of kinetic energy.

DAVID SR. Life is like a highway. If you can picture a highway during rush hour, no one moves more than a few feet per minute. We need jokes to decongest our minds from its load and tension. Then we relax and plan again our next hobbyhorse.

LINZI. Not until this whole episode of my family is over and the victory claimed. Then I'm gonna think about relaxing.

A hard knock is heard at the door.. Everybody is startled and looks in the direction of the door.

LINZI. [*Complaining.*] What? Who's crazy enough to be knocking hard as if he has the full right to knock on my door?

David Jr. goes toward the door. Just as he is about to open it, a second hard knock is heard.

DAVID JR. [*Startled as he open the door.*] Uncle Andricoco, is that you? [*Andricoco enters hurriedly.*] Are you okay, Uncle?

ANDRICOCO. [*He shows his badge to David Jr.*] I'm not your uncle now. I'm Officer Longfen. [*He shows a paper to David Jr.*] I'm on duty now. I gotta do what's in line with my duty. [*He looks at his paper, then at Lynette.*] You are Miss Lynnette Zibo, right?

LYNNETTE. Yes, sir, I am.

LINZI. [*Preoccupied.*] What's going on?

ANDRICOCO. [*Checking his paper and talking to Lynnette.*] What's your date of birth?

LYNNETTE. September ninth, two thousands nine.

ANDRICOCO. And your social?

LYNNETTE. Six oh oh eight oh nine six oh oh.

LINZI [*Very preoccupied.*] All this doesn't sound right.

ANDRICOCO. You've been indicted for the crime of forgery—

LINZI & DAVID JR. What? [*Lynnette and David Sr. are calm.*]

ANDRICOCO. —Which is a crime of the third degree here in Aerosanam—

LINZI. Forgery of what?

ANDRICOCO. Your bond is set at seventy-five thousand dollars.

LINZI & DAVID JR. What? Are you kidding? [*Lynnette and David Sr. are composed and do not react.*]

LINZI. [*To Andricoco.*] Brother, are you doing this to me? You putting yourself in the service of the devil, Arketta, against your own sister?

ANDRICOCO. [*To Linzi.*] I'm sorry, sister! I gotta do my job. I'm officially sent here. This is what I do to win my bread.

DAVID SR. You could recuse yourself.

ANDRICOCO. I did, but my boss said that I have to come get her or I'll get fired.

LINZI. If it's the bread that you looking for, I can provide it to you, anytime.

ANDRICOCO. I'm too old to be begging my sister's bread.

DAVID SR. Just go back and tell them that you didn't find her.

ANDRICOCO. [*To David Sr.*] No way. That'll be a breach of my professional commitment. [*To Lynnette.*] You need to get ready. I'm gonna take you to see the judge.

LYNNETTE. [*Calmly.*] I'm go like this.

LINZI. [*To Andricoco.*] Why you willing to pay for somebody else's sin? Arketta ain't worth dying for. I'm your sister, and I swear: I can die for you.

Up There to Step

Andricoco ignores Linzi and handcuffs Lynnette.

LINZI. Is this really happening? Brother, don't take her. That Arketta's trying to spark and fuel fire in my family. She's willing to divide you and me so she can reign. She's a Machiavellist.
DAVID JR. Take me instead of taking her, please. Alternatively, I request that I share Lynnette's prison cell.

Linzi's brow furrows. David Jr. makes silent inquiring gestures. Lynnette is sangfroid. Andricoco walks away with Lynnette toward the exit. There is a huge commotion in the family. David Jr. sobs. Linzi hugs and comforts him. David Sr. holds David Jr. by the hand and walks away with him, following behind Andricoco and Lynnette. They all exit. Linzi remains by herself in the living room. A spotlight falls on her as the stage goes dark.

LINZI. [*Reciting a poem.*]

> Ever since I was born,
> I've been enjoying life to its fullest extent.
> Life has given me all the joys of living
> Until when I moved to this town.
>
> Now, problems have overwhelmed me
> From left, right, north, south.
> I get no single respite in my dreams.
> I don't know what to do.
>
> The magic carpet that I'm riding was intended
> To help explore new worlds,
> To help me get away from some troubles,
> And to give me peace of mind and of heart.
> Why is it playing a counterwave game on me?

Peddar Panga

Is there any justice left in this world?
Is there any fairness, any truth left?
Is there any right to be claimed?
Is there any back on which to rely for rightness?

I cry for justice and order to be restored;
I cry for rightness to prevail over negativity;
I cry for peace over war and mutual destruction;
I cry for love to reign above every single matter.

I've been a victim of this cynical world.
I'm under the mercy of those who have tasted power,
Under the mercy of those who neglect the dignity of human
life,
Under the mercy of manipulators.

Why do some people ignore their humanity when they act?
Why do they forget that they are humans among other humans?
Why they ignore their human abilities and
Why they only hide behind their money?

Some humans, like Arketta, lie as they breathe.
Some humans, like Arketta, hurt as they smile.
Some humans, like Arketta, kill as they sleep.
Some humans, like Arketta, have only faith in their pockets.

People similar to Arketta strangely want to use invasive proce-
dures on poor men.
They increasingly want to fulfill their intensive greedy needs.
People similar to Arketta get richer by exploiting the poor.
They possess thousands of sheep,
But, they greedily wrest the last broken sheep of the poor.

Up There to Step

Why it has to be that it's only the law of the strongest
That needs to be always the best?
Can I get power to reverse this maxim?
Is there any magic potion I can make to bring changes about?

I stand now like King David in the Bible
With a small stone and a catapult.
I stand tall against the so-called almighty Goliath.
Will I prevail when my weapons are taken away from me?

Here I am, powerlessly witnessing the destruction of my dearest
son, David
This is not the way I intended him to be.
It's not on the nature of a great mother ~ as I am ~
To freakishly be reduced into a rotten worm

As the entire city of Aerosanam stands against me,
Against my family and my heart,
Against my pride and my soul,
Against my only and valued son, David.

If love is the strongest of all,
Why my sorrows and deception are winning over it?
Why power is knocking love down?
What needs to be done to restore the tarnished image of love?

God, please help me and my family.
We are being located in the mouth of the anaconda,
Waiting helplessly to be swallowed
In its own time.

Lights return on the stage.

DAVID SR. [*Enters, then pulls Linzi by her hand.*] Honey, let's go. We left already in the car and realized that we left you behind. We gotta go bail Lynnette out of jail. Let's go!

LINZI. How long have you been gone? I need more time to express my feelings to those walls. They are supposed to hear me. Those are the walls built with the sole purpose of safeguarding justice in this city.

DAVID SR. Let's go, baby! [*He pulls her, but she resists.*] Don't play the comedian here, please. There's no audience to give you a round of applause.

LINZI. Exactly! That's what I said!

Linzi walks away, hesitant, and they both exit.

Curtain.

SCENE 3

An altar is placed at the center of the stage. Antonio Moretti is a clergyman of a multidenominational Christian ministry. He is at home, wearing his clergy attire, a cassock. He is rehearsing the sermon he has to give to his followers at their next dominical meeting.

ANTONIO. [*Entering and laughing.*] Ha ha ha! God, I know 'ow to joke too. [*He gets to the stand, puts his Bible on top of it, and adjusts it.*] When I was writing dis sermon, you made me laugh to near death. [*Laughs.*] Do you want to 'ear my joke before I continue? Sure! I know you do, my God. [*He looks around.*] I 'ope nobody is spying on me. It will make 'im tink dat I am out of my mind. [*He adjusts himself.*] Okay, before I continue, here is my joke, Lord. God, please, take off your shoes; you know dat you standing on holy grounds. [*Laughs.*] Dis is not blasphemy, my God. It makes me feel like you and I are really connected good friends. [*Laughs.*] I know 'ow to joke too, my Lord. [*Laughs.*] Let us get serious now, my Lord. [*He takes a deep breath and becomes serious and composed.*] Before I rehearse dis sermon, a holy food dat you cooked for your people, let me say a prayer to invite you here in my house. [*He prays.*] Oh Lord, tank you for your word. Dis holy word dat existed at de beginning. Your word dat everybody has been plagiarizing to fit his own hunger for trut'. Your word dat I did not know dat it existed until de time you chose me to serve you as de shepherd for your flock of sheep. Tell me what to say to your children, Lord. Your love is always wit' me, and I tank you for your presence in my house.

[*He is rehearsing as if he were speaking to his church.*] Dere are many tings dat God cannot do. Dis is de title of our sermon today: "Tings dat God would not do."

[*He wipes his face with a handkerchief.*] Before I continue, allow me to remind you dat dis world has many opportunities and many doors to a brighter tomor-row. Wherever you step, dere are many more stairs on de ladder dat are up there to step. You hav-eh to walk dem by yourself. God may help you only if you can first help yourself. [*Pause.*] God cannot do many tings. I hav-eh a list of tings dat God cannot do. Let me first give you de list, and later I will explain each point particularly. [*He clears his throat.*] Dis list is not exhaustive:

One, God cannot be prejudiced.
Two, God cannot break a promise.
Tree, God cannot sleep.
Four, God cannot lie.
Five, God cannot remember sins he chose to forgive.
Six, God cannot lose or fail.
Seven, God cannot stop loving you. If you are hungry, he will give you your daily bread. And—

A hard knock is heard at the door. Antonio stops rehearsing. He looks in the direction of the door,, very surprised. Betsy enters, broadly smiling, and walks straight to where Antonio is standing. She stops closer to him. Her pregnant belly touches Antonio.

BETSY. I'm hungry, and I got no penny on me.
ANTONIO. [*He steps away from her and speaks calmly.*] Do I know you?
BETSY. You don't need to know me in order to help me.
ANTONIO. Keep dat advice to yourself. I do not want to hear it.
BETSY. I haven't ate anything yet and I don't have money.
ANTONIO. And you want me to give you and de food and de money?
BETSY. I'm really hungry and penniless. Someone in your neighborhood told me to come here 'cause you a minister of God and you can help me.
ANTONIO. Go work or go apply for food stamps and de WIC—
BETSY. I already applied for food stamps and for the Woman, Infant, and Child program. But the help I get ain't enough to last till the next supply. Since I got pregnant, I've been a gourmand, eating like a pig. It's some sort of unexplained craving for food that my doctors are unable to fix. [*She tries to step closer to him. He stops her with a hand gesture.*] I can't work, Father. The baby I'm carrying has turned me into a sleeping machine.

ANTONIO. [*He looks at her feet.*] Take your shoes off, please. Dis place is kind of holy. I'm rehearsing my sermon. I invited God in here already. So take your shoes off, please.

BETSY. [*Smiling.*] Is that a joke?

ANTONIO. [*Angrily, he raises his voice.*] You are de joke. Do you know dat what you just did is a spiritual crime, a blasphemy? [*Betsy shakes her head.*] Well, you should know. [*Betsy frowns and puts her arms in a forty-five-degree angle, palms upward in a sign of interrogation.*] If you knew what you just did, seducing a holy man in a holy place and disrupting his rehearsal, you would not hav-eh risked your life. [*Sighs.*] If you were sent by de devil, tell 'im dat he has de wrong person to tempt. I'm shielded by God's love.

BETSY. [*With a pleading tone.*] Please, Father, I didn't come here with bad intents. I'm just fulfilling Jesus's advice. He said ask and you shall be given. I'm hungry and want something to eat. That's all.

ANTONIO. [*With firm nervousness.*] When your time of labor approaches, you will climb up a tree, you will throw yourself on de ground like a chameleon, and your belly will explode. Dat is De way you will deliver.

BETSY. [*Disturbed.*] Why is that? Why are you cursing me?

ANTONIO. Becaus-eh you hav-eh seduced a holy man rehearsing in de presence of de Lord.

BETSY. [*Piteously.*] I didn't seduce you, father. I'm just hungry and looking for some to eat. How could it be that I seduced you while all I need and ask for is food?

ANTONIO. You touched your sinful belly to my holy body. You invaded my personal space. You aroused me.

BETSY. [*With delight.*] Only for that, you cursed me, really?

ANTONIO. [*Energetically.*] You cursed yourself.

BETSY. [*Sweetly.*] That ain't a Christian thing to do, Father. You acting against Jesus's examples. When a bleeding woman touched him, he told her that her faith had healed her. You could've told me that my faith has healed my hunger, my craving, or better. Or just give me something to eat or tell me to go 'cause you've got none. [*Pause.*] But a poor woman comes to look for food, and you telling her that she'll deliver by bursting her belly up?

ANTONIO. [*Pointing.*] Let me tell you someting, lady. You will go to hell after you die of your sins during your delivery.

BETSY. Hell? [*She laughs and shakes her head.*] I can't go to no hell. I ain't fit for hell. I'm so naturally soft and fearful. Ever since I was born, I never even went to a gym. I never worked out. Hell ain't designed for people like me. It fits people who possess hard-rock hearts like yours. People like you can adapt in hell easily. I ain't designed for hell. I ain't able to survive in hell.

ANTONIO. In dat case, you should not be playing de whore. You should not be walking around fulfilling your dad, de devil's mission. It's like buying an express ticket to hell. It does not mat-ter if you are fit for hell or not.

BETSY. [*She rubs her belly.*] I'm hungry. [*Strongly.*] I'll tell you what: you the one who'll go to hell for ignoring to help me.

ANTONIO. [*Normally.*] You came to me to tell me how I'll go hell?

BETSY. I came to beg for support, but you cursed me instead.

ANTONIO. [*Innocently.*] I cannot curse you. I'm God's minister. I bless people. I do not curse dem.

BETSY. [*Insistently.*] You did curse me.

ANTONIO. Me?

BETSY. [*Big sigh.*] Well, you just forgot what you told me a couple minutes ago? You condemned me for begging you for food, and you sentenced me to death like a chameleon and to damnation in hell.

ANTONIO. [*Calmly.*] You talking about someone else.

BETSY. If you denying what you just told me, then you a liar. I wonder why you call your house a holy place when you can curse and lie the same way you breathe.

ANTONIO. I'm impressed. Really impressed. You came to beg for support, den you are giving me a hard time?

BETSY. You don't need to be impressed. Jesus himself, who was a son of God, was born, and nobody was impressed. Only you? [*Sigh.*] I'm the one who's really impressed. Really impressed to meet someone like you. People like you, I call them white beans. This's the second time in my life I've met a white bean. They shut their doors before opening them to the needy, and they claim to be God's fervent servitors.

ANTONIO. [*Fiercely.*] My ministry is a vocation. God chose me to serve as a shepherd. If you doubt it, go hang yourself.

BETSY. Well! [*Deep breath.*] Before I decide to go hang myself, I'd love to see a priest preaching naked like in the story of the emperor's new clothes. I'd like to see a giant priest, naked, preaching, with a small penis. It'll be less of an abomination. I don't want to see the kind of priest who curses and condemns a hungry lady but pretends to be holy and in the presence of God. It sounds very controversial to me.

ANTONIO. Lady, you are de one who came to me. I did not invite you here. If you did come here all dis could not be happening... seriously... You disrupted my sermon rehearsal... You were and still are de devil's messenger.... I will help you return to hell, where you belong... You curse yourself for entering a holy place wit' shoes. You soiled my place. You brought negative vibrations from hell, where your father, de devil, sent you to seduce me. I hav-eh a message for him. You can deliver it to him when you go back. Tell your father, Lucifer, dat he cannot hav-eh me.

BETSY. [*Calmly.*]I ain't from hell. I've got no message to deliver to the devil. Hell is for strong people. [*Pause.*] Like you. I'm too weak for hell. I don't qualify to be a hell citizen. But you do. I ain't cranked enough to sustain hell.

ANTONIO. You are from hell becaus-eh de devil sent you to seduce me. His temptations won't work here.

BETSY. Job, in the Bible, was able to successfully sustain the devil's long and disastrous temptations for many days. Jesus also, after forty days of fasting, successfully warded off the devil's temptations. But you, you claim to almost have failed to honor my demand for food only 'cause my belly touched you? Are you really a God servant? If yes, you could only entertain the positive side of every equation or temptation, as you call it.

ANTONIO. I hav-eh realized dat people take advantage of me for being friendly. Dey abuse my good heart.

BETSY. If you claim to have a big heart, you shouldn't be giving me a hard time, 'cause I asked you for food.

ANTONIO. De devil comes disguised in many ways. He may take de form of a beggar or of a pregnant woman pretending to be hungry. I know de way he works.

BETSY. You still calling me the devil? Where did you get that fathead energy to curse God's creatures like that? You making it easy as if you were in control of my destiny. Your so-called holy curse will go back to you. Lemme remind you what the Bible says. I quote: "God is not mocked."

ANTONIO. You are trying to steal my show while I'm rehearsing my sermon. So get out of here, devil.

BETSY. [*Nodding.*] Those last words just sparked some hard memories in me. The same statements were spoken to me by a guy who checkmated me on the back his car. He gave me the wrong business card. I think you should be the guy responsible for the embarrassment that my belly is undergoing. [*Pause.*] Tell me, priest, are you the father of the baby I'm carrying? I've found you by chance.

ANTONIO. I cannot be your baby father becaus-eh I am gay. I never been wit' a woman.

BETSY. If you deny it, I'll take you to court to get your DNA checked.

ANTONIO. Go to your court if you want, but get out of here, devil.

BETSY. [*She starts walking toward the exit.*] Now that your greediness has warmed you up, you gonna have a great day. Enjoy the rest of your rehearsal.

Curtain.

SCENE 4
In David Sr.'s living room. Curtain opens. Kassandra walks in, going in the direction of the coffee table.

KASSANDRA. I hate men. When they come back home, they go sit on the couch and stretch out their feet. They don't care that there are dishes in the kitchen or a bed to make or even a trash bag to dump. [*She picks up her cell phone, lying on the table. She checks the screen and complains.*] Nobody called me today! I can't believe it. What's wrong? [*She verifies the network.*] I'm connected to the network, and my service is on. But I can't believe that I haven't received any single call since this morning and—[*She looks at her watch.*] It's six p.m. Oh God! [*She dials a number.*] Lemme call this guy and see if my phone's working. [*The phone rings, and she speaks.*] Hey!

PHONE [*Voice of Jevus*]. Hallo, honey!

KASSANDRA. Where are you at?

PHONE [*Voice of Jevus*]. I am chasin' all de elephants up here.

KASSANDRA: What?

PHONE [*Voice of Jevus*]. I am just playin' around here.

KASSANDRA: I heard something else.

PHONE [*Voice of Jevus*]. What did you hear?

KASANDRA. Just tell me where you are at, please.

PHONE [*Voice of Jevus*]. [*Yelling.*] I told jou where I was. Did jou forget?

KASSANDRA. [*Raising her voice.*] Stop yelling at me, or I'm gonna toss this phone into the wall.

PHONE [*Voice of Jevus*]. I am not djellin'. I put jou on speaker because I am crossin' a school zone. It is a hand-free zone. My phone is on my lap. To talk to you, I have to talk very loud.

KASSANDRA. [*Normally.*] I know you better. You never miss an argument to defend yourself when in trouble.

PHONE [*Voice of Jevus*]. I was at my friend's place, remember? I told jou that he had an accident.

KASSANDRA. You'd better hurry up here. I'm hungry. Come cook for me, please.

PHONE [*Voice of Jevus*]. I will be there shortly. Bye!

A female voice is heard on Jevus's line, arguing with Jevus.

PHONE [*Female voice*]. Is that all?
PHONE [*Voice of Jevus*]. What? ¿Lo que está hablando?
PHONE [*Female voice*]. That's your wife, right?
PHONE [*Voice of Jevus*]. So?
PHONE [*Female voice*]. You hung up on your wife so briskly?
PHONE [*Voice of Jevus*]. Get to de point, please.
PHONE [*Female voice*]. You should have said words like "I love you," or just any loving formula before you hung up.
PHONE [*Voice of Jevus*]. *Lociento!* I am not from here. I have to learn.
KASSANDRA [*She is still listening to the conversation. Now she yells.*] What? Jevus, you riding with a hooker in my car?
PHONE [*Voice of Jevus*]. Jou are wrong, baby! Dat is the radio.
KASSANDRA. The radio talking to you? I heard a voice of a female bitch giving you lessons how to hang up your phone with your wife.
PHONE [*Voice of Jevus*]. It was just a coincidence. It was two radio announcers havin' a conversation about that subject. I am alone in the car.
KASSANDRA. [*Normally.*] I know you! You were vaccinated against defeat. You always find alibis even when caught on the spot.
PHONE [*Voice of Jevus*]. I don't know what jou are talkeen about.
KASSANDRA. Go away! Anyway, fine! [*She hangs up her phone and complains to herself.*] The phone's working. But I never had a day like this when nobody calls me all day long. [*She throws her hands in the air.*] Anyway, whatever.

On TV, a game is playing. Kassandra sits on the couch and takes the remote control. As soon as she takes it, David Jr. enters and commands her.

DAVID JR. You better not touch—
KASSANDRA. [*Jumping and laughing after a slight shock.*] Eh, David—
DAVID JR. That TV. I'm watching the game.

KASSANDRA. You scared the hell out of me.
DAVID JR. I didn't mean to scare you, but I need to watch my game.
KASSANDRA. [*Standing up.*] Okay. I'm gonna go to my room then.

Kassandra stands up and walks exits the scene. David Jr. sits down and raises the volume of the TV. Several seconds later, Jevus enters.

JEVUS. Eh, David.
DAVID JR. [*He doesn't move.*] Eh!
JEVUS. Who is playeen?
DAVID JR. The Squatch versus the Magbonja. You probably don't know those football teams, do you?
JEVUS. Well, Aerosanam Football? *Nunca* watched it. I do not even know the rules. Anyway, who is winning?
DAVID JR. The game's tied.
JEVUS. Already?
DAVID JR. [*He raises his voice up, yelling.*] Why you say "already" as if there's a winner? Game tied means no team is winning so far.
JEVUS. Come on, boy! Seriously, jou need to djell at me for dat? *¿Por qué no le gusto mí?*
DAVID JR. [*He speaks angrily.*] Me to like you?...Why should I?
JEVUS. Oh my God, anoder day, anoder trouble! *Soy su cuñado*, not your enemy.
DAVID JR. Just don't come around here trying to stab my feelings. I've got a lot going on in my life right now, and don't add more, please. I don't wanna hear anybody talking to me right now.
JEVUS. I know the cure to jour trouble, boy. I have to make you kiss jour own *culo*. When it happens, let me know. I can put it into the Guinness World Records.
DAVID JR. You know that I can kill you in a minute if you don't stop talking to me, do you?
JEVUS. Do jou hear jourself, how jou sound? Dat is de same way jour grandpa used to sound. He used to say someteeng like dis. [*He mimics a very funny voice and makes hand gestures.*] "Bring me nine additional workers.

Because of low performance, I dumped de seven you sent me djesterday in the water. Dey died by drowning." [*With his normal voice.*] Jour mentality of domination—when will it end?

DAVID JR. [*He stands to face Jevus, cussing.*] Go away, you! You acting like a singing mosquito.

JEVUS. Jou are the one who chould go away. See how jou look like a wet Jesus.

DAVID JR. [*Normally, nodding his head.*] Fortunately, you know to speak. I'm so delighted. However, you know what happens to a toddler when he learns to speak? He can say anything. That's what's become of you, a toddler.

JEVUS. I am a toddler, me? Then jou are an infant.

DAVID JR. [*Raising his voice.*] Stop it and shut your ass up. [*Deep breath.*] You getting under my skin now.

JEVUS. I have to get under jour fuckeen skin because jou are evil like jour ancestors.

KASSANDRA. [*Entering and yelling.*] Guys, stop it. [*David Jr. and Jevus stop cussing at each other and look at Kassandra.*] Why you guys never got along?

JEVUS. Dis guy do not like me. He said it very loud.

KASSANDRA. Eh, David! Love your brother-in-law like you love your sister, please!

DAVID JR. What? You usually against me in favor of your husband.

KASSANDRA. You were yelling. I heard you first.

DAVID JR. You should be on my side. You know I been going through a very hard time the last three weeks, and you adding more to my fuckin' pain, right? I'd at least have peace here, in my house.

KASSANDRA. I know our family has been very supportive to you since this crisis started. And you are not the only one affected. All the family is grieving for your misfortune. However, I beg you to like your brother-in-law. I, your sister, was made out of his ribs. So love thy sister, David. Why are you cussing with hue and cry that you don't love him?

DAVID JR. [*Enraged, he throws the TV remote control on the couch.*] Now, sister, today is the day. Every time there's tension between your ugly husband and me, you never been on my side. Now, today is the day. You gotta decide, between me and your husband, who is your pick?

JEVUS. [*He walks to the opposite side of Kassandra, who is now standing between the two men.*] Yeah! I would love to know. Let us see, between jour husband and jour broder, who is jour pick?

KASSANDRA. [*Negotiating.*] Come on, guys. You don't need to put me under this great two-thousand-year-old dilemma. I know Jesus was asked by one of his followers what should be the choice between burying his father and following Jesus. Jesus told him to leave the dead, bury the dead. Now, on this case, I'm gonna solve this dilemma my way. I pick both of you. You are both so valuable to me.

DAVID JR. You better not. If you choose both of us, you lose me forever.

JEVUS. Same goes with me. If jou pick both of us, jou lose me forever.

KASSANDRA. I really don't wanna do this. But you guys are pushing me to the extreme. Now you can see the blood going to my head. [*She looks at Jevus.*] You've made so many kids before you married me. You are dangerous. I don't trust you. But you are the wanted evil. I can't let you go, 'cause I need you, the evil, to help me face the other most evil part of myself, me. [*She walks toward Jevus.*]

JEVUS. [*Nodding and making provocative faces at David Jr.*] I knew it, boy! And I told jou! I know jour sister better than herself. So go kiss de devil's ass.

Jevus opens his hands to welcome and hug Kassandra as she walks slowly toward him. David Jr. is standing steadily, watching with no emotion. Suddenly, Kassandra stops three feet away from Jevus.

KASSANDRA. [*Shaking her finger.*] Blood is thick than water. You know what I mean, man? You're out of blood. You're of no use to the vampire that I am. [*She walks back toward David Jr.*] I pick you, brother. You are my bloody brother. [*She hugs David Jr. and points at Jevus.*] I can replace a husband in a minute. But a brother? Well, the choice's clear.

David Jr. is contented. He laughs and points at Jevus with mockery. Jevus is looking with eyes wide open, dumbfounded.

DAVID JR. [*Laughing.*] You are the one who looks like a wet Jesus now. [*Both Kassandra and David Jr. laugh at him.*]
JEVUS. [*Snapping out of it.*] I will tell jou what, David. Jour sister has been causeen you all the misery that jou are goin' through against dat Iron Lady of Arleta. I have overheard her multiple times talkeen to the people in Arleta's circle. She has been giveen dem all jour information, all jour moves, everything, including de decisions dat were made in this house. So tell me, is that a true sister or just a vampire who is sellin' her own brother's blood?

Both David Jr. and Kassandra are startled. They release their hold and look at each other. Kassandra shakes her head as David Jr. opens his hands, asking for an explanation.

JEVUS. [*Continuing triumphantly.*] Remember de oder day at de airport? She stayed behind everybody and was reporteen de arrival of jour girlfriend, Lynnette. Dat is why Arleta's circle arranged to get her arrested and forfeit jour wedding ceremony. Dat is not all. Ask her where she found de money to bail Lynnette out of jail. Ask her. Where did she find de seventy-five dousand dollars for de bond? She paid it out of her pocket. Where did she get de money? She does not work. It is just de money she gets paid for sellin' jou and jour family. Now, if she picks you, she is just tryin' to cover her butt. She does not love you.

David Jr. wants to explode. Kassandra attacks Jevus. She pulls at his shirt.

KASSANDRA. [*Repeating.*] You liar! You liar! You liar!

DAVID JR. [*To Kassandra.*] So was it you, sister? Tell me, please! Was it you all along? I knew that there was somebody leaking information from this house. I was suspecting your husband. But was it you?

KASSANDRA. [*She stops attacking Jevus and looks at David Jr.*] I don't know what he's talking about. He's a liar. Don't believe him.

DAVID JR. How come Arketta always knows what's going on in this house? How come she can specifically say every single word we spoke in this house? How come she controls my moves? [*No answer.*] I got you. You see? A thief will only hide for forty days. On the forty-first day, he'll get caught. Now I've spotted you, spy sister.

Kassandra is speechless. She sobs, approaches David Jr., and drops to her knees.

DAVID JR. [*Pushing Kassandra away.*] Starting today, you are no longer my sister. I also warn you that you need to stop spying on me. If I hear any other leak from my life, just be prepared for the consequences. What I'll do to you, you'll blame nobody other than yourself.

David Jr. walks away from Kassandra and exits the scene.

KASSANDRA. [*She stays on her knees and stretches her hand in the David's direction, crying..*] He's a liar! David, don't go before you learn the truth. Jevus is a liar. I don't know none of what he just said. I'm innocent.

A couple seconds later, Jevus, who was still contemplating his successful move, advances and holds Kassandra. She responds positively. She stands up and hugs Jevus.

JEVUS. Even if jour broder denies jou, remember, a husband is supposed to share the rest of his life with you.

KASSANDRA. [*Sadly.*] Why are you doing this to me? Why you lied to my brother? You know he may seek revenge and probably kill me, an innocent sister.

JEVUS. It was a war. I was supposed to use every strategy to win it. I was not ready to helplessly witness my love to my wife bein' melted in from on me. Jou choud have just understood dat I am not ready to lose my wife in favor of my broder-in-law.

KASSANDRA. Are you fuckin' serious?

JEVUS. You asked me to iron jour shoes, instead of jour clothes. I said yes. *Pero* who will be de loser? Have jou ever seen anybody ironing shoes?

KASSANDRA. If you love me, you don't have to lie. 'Cause we're on the same team.

JEVUS. Jou have been watcheen my belly instead of watcheen my back. Dat is why.

KASSANDRA. That's why you sparking fire between me and my brother?

JEVUS. He tried to separate me from my lovely wife. Bein' alive is a full-time war. I am not a coward, and I am supposed to have the courage to fight as a full-time employee of my family, on a twenty-four-hour basis.

KASSANDRA. I've nothing to do with spying on my brother. Maybe somebody else does it. Not me. The money with which I bailed Lynnette out—it's from my last marriage. I saved a lot of money from my divorce. You probably don't understand how you added more fire to the existing fire in our family. [*Sigh.*] Did you even weigh your accusations against your own wife? What do you think about my family's reaction? Mom, Dad— how do you think they'll react when David tells them that I spy on him?

JEVUS. I will tell dem dat I lied. It was just in order to save my love. Love today is tinier than de eye of a needle. I would not let it go easily, because I may not be able to fit in the eye of the next needle.

KASSANDRA. You went to an extreme. I'm afraid that David'll never recover from this.

JEVUS. Jou pushed me into this. Jou and jour brother were makin' fun of me. Besides, I was paralyzed and losin' love. I felt that jou were suckin' and emptyin' my love to jou so fast dat I was obliged to counter. Love is like a knife in the hands of a baby. Just be careful to take it away from him to avoid damage.

KASSANDRA. Now find ways to convince my brother to reconcile with me. I'm afraid of his vengeance against me.

JEVUS. I will make sure dat everyteen goes as smoothly as before. *Pero* I do have an advice for jou. Let's jour sweet voice shine—let it vibrate. Let its babyish sound massage my tympani, my brain, and my heart. Let jour angelic voice cure me from doin' wrong to jou.

KASSANDRA. [*She smiles and sweetens her voice.*] I love you.

JEVUS. I love jou too.

Hugs and kisses follow.

KASSANDRA. You always needed money to take care of your family back home, right? Here's what you need now. [*She gives to him a couple bills.*]

Jevus closes his mouth.

KASSANDRA. You can't say thanks?

JEVUS [...]

KASSANDRA. Thanks for no thanks.

Curtain.

SCENE 5

At Arleta's place. In the living room, Arleta's a special chair, like a throne, placed on a carpet.

> *Curtain opens. Arketta, disguised as Arleta, is sitting in the special chair. Kalol, one of her female servants, enters with Antonio Moretti, the priest. When they get closer to Arleta's chair, Kalol introduces the visitor.*

KALOL. [*She bows.*] Mother, here's the visitor.

Arketta smiles greatly. She stays seated. Kalol bows again and leaves. Antonio remains standing.

ARKETTA. [*Laughing.*] Who vested you like this?
ANTONIO. What do you mean, madam? I am a priest. I dress like dis.
ARKETTA. Did you wear this whole uniform just to get paid minimum wage, or you just wanted to impress me?
ANTONIO. I do not get paid per hour, and it is not minimum wage. I am God's minister. Most of my rewards for serving God will be in paradise.
ARKETTA. How many pounds does your uniform weigh?
ANTONIO. None. I never paid attention. Why do you want to know?
ARKETTA. The uniform looks funny and makes you look funny too, like a clown.
ANTONIO. I am a clown in de service of de Lord.
ARKETTA. Is there any prestige that comes with being a clown?
ANTONIO. Yeah, an overrated prestige!
ARKETTA. Well, I can tell. [*Pause.*] You knocked on my bungalow to ask for Halloween candy, trick or treat, or is there something else on the line?
ANTONIO. I am de priest you hired for your wedding ceremony.
ARKETTA. Ah, I see! You are Antonio Moretti, right? I thought you sealed the deal with Mr. Kapoza, my servant and the lawyer of my daughter, Arketta. Something went wrong? I usually don't work directly with people. I got a bunch of people that I pay to carry out my orders.

ANTONIO. I hav-eh a special message; that's why I requested dis special audience.

ARKETTA. Okay! What brought you to my bungalow today? How can I help you?

ANTONIO. Do you know why Jesus died?

ARKETTA. Is he dead already?

ANTONIO. Well, I mean he is alive, but he died for your sins. Do you know dat?

ARKETTA. He's alive, but he died for my sins? You're confusing me. Somebody can't be dead and be alive at the same time. Is that your way of saying the truth?

ANTONIO. Jesus is de begotten son of God. As de son of God, he is God too. But he accepted to wear a body and be incarnated as man in order to save your life.

ARKETTA. To save my life?

ANTONIO. You do not need to go to hell if you accept Jesus.

ARKETTA. You're confusing me. You mix sin, life, hell, and I don't know where my piece of the cake is.

ANTONIO. If you accept Jesus, your sins will be cleansed. Jesus died for that purpose. Den you will hav-eh your life saved. You will not go to hell, but you will go to heaven after you die. It is a great and free deal, but dere is just one responsibility on your part. You hav-eh to avoid sin. Moreover, if you sin, you hav-eh to ask Jesus for forgiveness. [*Pause.*] Do you accept Jesus as your savior, madam?

ARKETTA. Are you sure you are at the right lion's den? Who invited you here? Or better, who told you that I needed a priest here?

ANTONIO. I follow God's directions, madam. God sent me here to deliver dis special message to you.

ARKETTA. And God told you to come to minister me 'cause I'm a sinner?

ANTONIO. Yeah, kind of, becaus-eh everybody is a sinner. And so I am. But I accepted Jesus as my savior. He accepted to redeem all my iniquities.

ARKETTA. God sent you to me, you said, right?

ANTONIO. Sure, he did.

ARKETTA. What name God gave you?

ANTONIO. Arleta Yavanov.

ARKETTA. What kind of sin did God tell you that Arleta has committed?

ANTONIO. David. Do you know David?

ARKETTA. Which one?

ANTONIO. David Schumerman.

ARKETTA. [*Delighted and nodding.*] Ah! Now I see. Why you believe to be a minister of God but you lie in his name? Is it a new way of sinning without being held accountable?

ANTONIO. I did not lie, madam.

ARKETTA. It's clear and obvious that David Schumerman Sr. or his wife sent you here to convince me to get away from his son, right? And you lied to me that it's God who sent you here. [*She shakes her head.*] David and Linzi have been a pain in my neck ever since I loved their son. Can't they leave me alone? They've unsuccessfully tried everything to get me away from their son, but it never worked. Today, they sent me a minister to lie to me that God sent him. Why're you lying in the name of God?

ANTONIO. It is a sin to force a boy who is de age of your great-grandson to marry you. Your acts are going against de Ten Commandments of God.

ARKETTA. Wait a minute. God told you that it's a sin for a lady to marry a young boy?

ANTONIO. You are way too old for David. Will you really be able to open your legs for 'im? Dat will be like cursing de boy. You will be with de boy, sucking his humanity and destroying his life.

ARKETTA. First off, I'm not old. Second off, God told me to marry David.

ANTONIO. You need to be sure dat de voice you heard was dat of God. You cannot select an alternative that is unheard of. Otherwise, it is going to be de greatest abomination since de deluge era.

ARKETTA. You need to tell me that God, my God, lied to me?

ANTONIO. God, our God, de true God, cannot send you to go to sin.

ARKETTA. Marriage isn't a sin. It's a holy matrimonial union.

ANTONIO. If it is a holy union, why are you forcing de boy into it? He is so immature. He is not ready for a wife yet, and he has been refusing your advances using all his limited strategies, but you hav-eh wasted your fortune to keep forcing him without his consent.

ARKETTA. I told you that it was God's voice urging me to marry that boy. I'll go with that even if it means de destruction of de boy, as you claim.

ANTONIO. You are confused, madam. I am going to deliver you from de evil spirits dat possess you, in de name of Jesus.

ARKETTA. Boy, lemme remind you that you getting into my ass. You're very lucky to be talking to me, 'cause many are denied that chance. I'm seventy years old. I know all the bullshit that comes my way. I'm able to raise hell. However, I can't raise it against you. But, believe me, I do know how to.

ANTONIO. I hav-eh been preaching for eighteen years. I was under de impression that I hav-eh seen it all. But I never ran across dis. God telling a seventy-year-old lady to force into marriage a seventeen-year-old boy? I don't care if dere are walls and stupid people around; but, I wonder to know when you can go in three seconds or what you can you do in one minutes. Dere is no truth anymore. Dere is no hope. Everyting is falling in de darkness because-eh of people like you.

ARKETTA. [*Laughing.*] Is that speaking in new tongues? I guess the Holy Spirit has visited you, 'cause what you say doesn't make sense anymore. If you elect to suck Jesus to his bone, which one'll get to your mouth the fastest? Your lies or your Jesus?

ANTONIO. God sent me to do dis job. I am ready to die, if that is de will of God. I am ready to die in order to deliver you from your sins. You are possessed by evil spirits. And everybody in Aerosanam is sick and tired of you. I hav-eh to save you.

ARKETTA. Oh come on. You didn't come here to save me, boy. What I see in your eyes is the same attitude that Torquemada had during the Inquisition in Europe. He believed he was sent by God to torture those who were reported to have stepped aside from the Bible. He and many other inquisitors had the blessing of the highest authority of the Christian church. They believed that 'cause Jesus died for many, they had to force the heretics, especially Jews, to salvation. [*Slight pause.*] You trying to force me to confess to sins you believe I did, that I ain't aware of. You and Torquemada are the same. You may be his clone.

ANTONIO. You cannot know how disappointed I am, madam. You cannot compare me to de inquisitors; I am God's humble servant.

ARKETTA. I'm God's humble servant, too. And I'm telling the truth. Torquemada believed to be God's humble servant too.

ANTONIO. If you claim to be God's servant, why you hav-eh de mark of de devil on your face?

ARKETTA. [*She laughs.*] You tell me, please. There're big horns on top of your head. Are they the mark of God?

ANTONIO. [*He passes a hand over the top of his head.*] Well, I will tell you de truth: you are a servant of de devil. You do not want to be applying for hell citizenship while you are alive.

ARKETTA. If the devil is a hell citizen, why does he have an American name?

ANTONIO. What is his name?

ARKETTA. You tell me! You've been talking to me about hell and about de devil since you came here. You'd give even a deaf person the great impression that you know the devil. [*Slight pause.*] Please describe to me how hell is and what the devil looks like. It seems like you've been there and you know who he is.

ANTONIO. Hell is in every store. What do you tink hell is, madam?

ARKETTA. You can't tell me to describe hell. I've got no idea what it is. [*Silence.*] I've heard that it's kind of a lake of fire that burns, but I don't know exactly what hell is. [*Sigh.*] Listen to me. I provide the highest loving experience, more than anybody else around this town. That's one of my express tickets to heaven. I have nothing to worry about hell.

ANTONIO. Jesus said don't be contented becaus-eh you do miracles, but be contented if your name is written in de book of life.

ARKETTA. Your same Jesus said that only charity will take you to heaven. I spend billions of my money on charities; I'm worthy to go to heaven.

ANTONIO. You may be filled with a good giving heart, but, because-eh of your blindness, you may keep destroying your good giving acts. Jesus said if you give with one hand, do not let your other hand know. But, you spent your life giving and singing songs for anyone to hear that you are de greatest giver that de world has ever seen. Den you run amok, using your giving nature as a power tool to control, destroy, and crush anybody in your path. You are just hurting yourself. You cannot go to heaven after destroying your charitable actions by your own wrongdoings.

ARKETTA [*Smiling.*] I have read the story Don Quixote De la Mancha. [*Chuckling.*] You sound really like him.

ANTONIO. You are a female, madam, but de only problem is that you ignore it. You ignore yourself.

ARKETTA. I've proven that a woman is stronger than anything you just said.

ANTONIO. Keep lying to yourself. Your pride ends where man starts—

ARKETTA. I'm gonna defy the common myth that claims out loud that man was created before woman. The truth is, woman was created first, and man was pulled out of woman's ribs.

ANTONIO. I hav-eh hard time understanding you.

ARKETTA. Adam, the first created human, was a woman. She was black too. Eve was a man. We've been taught to believe the contrary. I can demonstrate with supporting facts what I'm saying.

ANTONIO. That's not what de Bible says.

ARKETTA. In the Bible, it's said that Barabbas was acquitted and Jesus was condemned. That's wrong. The truth is, Jesus was dismissed and Barabbas was condemned.

ANTONIO. You mean to tell me dat de Bible lied?

ARKETTA. Don't put words in my mouth. I didn't say that the Bible lied.

ANTONIO. I heard you saying someting that is not written in de Bible.

ARKETTA. You making yourself a lawyer of the Bible? In that case, go sue every Bible user, 'cause each Bible comes with a different version and a different understanding of a given verse and chapter. There're many sects based on a different understanding of the truth of a biblical line. You got the cure?

ANTONIO. Regardless, if you say that Jesus was acquitted, you're blaspheming. Jesus was condemned, and he died for you. He is de reason I am here for you.

ARKETTA. I'm the one who has to save you and your Jesus.

ANTONIO. With all due respect, I am afraid I hav-eh to confirm that you are possessed by demons. Your delusions say it loud. I hav-eh to save you unless you want to go to hell.

ARKETTA. Me?

ANTONIO. Yes. You will go to hell.

ARKETTA. I wanna ask you a favor, priest. Can you go to hell on my behalf?

ANTONIO. What?

ARKETTA. You've been in my head for so long. I want you to go to hell on my behalf. I'll pay you for that.

ANTONIO. Why?

ARKETTA. 'Cause you've been lying in the name of God.

ANTONIO. Me lying? I came to reproach you for lying in de name of God. I want to save you from going to hell. It is my job. God chose me to save souls from eternal damnation in de name of Jesus.

ARKETTA. In your pot, only lies are boiling.

ANTONIO. God sent me to talk to you. To warn you against your own destruction.

ARKETTA. I see your weakness. It just take money to put you away.

ANTONIO. I hate to talk about money, politics, and sex.

ARKETTA. I've a little confession for you, for your pleasure. I want to make you happy. Until now, you've been taught and have learned love, compassion, and all kinds of positivity. Starting today, you have to learn deception, hate, and negativity, in order to be balanced in the future. We need balance in life in order to survive the shock of the unpredictable. The heart needs to be trained in both case scenarios.

ANTONIO. I care a lot about balance, becaus-eh you are acting against social equilibrium. God sent me where chaos reigns to reestablish balance.
ARKETTA. [*Laughing.*] Let's see, between you and me, who's really lying in the name of God. I ain't gonna drive you out. You'll be driven out by yo'self. [*She claps her hands.*]

Arleta, the mother, the true Arleta, enters. The priest is startled.

ARKETTA. [*Taking off her wig and some of her makeup.*] Mr. the clown priest! Lemme introduce you to the true Arleta Yavanov, my mother.
ARLETA. [*Walking toward Antonio.*] Another blind hit-up lie in the name of God?
ARKETTA. [*To the priest.*] If I were you, wearing that uniform again would gimme a nightmare.
ARLETA. If God really sent you here, why he failed to reveal to you that you were talking to the fake Arleta Yavanov? Do you see how you guys always lie in the name of the almighty God?

Antonio is speechless. Arleta walks around him twice.

ARLETA. Close your eyes and tell me what you see.
ANTONIO. [*He closes his eyes.*] Nothing.
ARLETA, Yeah! That's all we are, blind. We can't even see as far as the tip of our nose.

Antonio is still speechless, prompting Arleta to keep talking with a dominating (bullying) attitude.

ARLETA. Gimme your hand.
ANTONIO. What?
ARLETA. I'm asking for your hand.
ANTONIO. Why, do you wanna marry me?

ARLETA. I didn't say that I wanna marry you. Can you show me your hand, please?

ANTONIO. Okay. Next time, do not say, "I am asking your hand," becaus-eh in dis country, that expression means to ask someone for marriage. [*He stretches his right hand toward Arleta.*]

ARLETA. [*She looks at his hand for a second and releases it.*] This is probably your lucky day. Arleta has a reputation of a destroyer. Not a criminal. I can expose you to the public for all the adventures you've been digging around in your parish for the last sixteen years. You've impregnated many married women in the name of your faith. I know every single kid you made, and I can prove it easily. Those kids are living with dads that they believe to be their fathers, but in reality, you are their biological father. You've slept with so many women of your parish, and they think you're a celebrity. Many are seduced by the way you preach, and the next thing they realize is that they're in your bed, sleeping with a man who is supposed to cleanse them of their sins. Anyway, you are lucky today 'cause I'm gonna let you go. I'm not gonna explore your weakness that you believe to be your strength. But I warn you to not attempt to refuse to officiate my wedding ceremony. It may cost your life. Do you understand?

Antonio nods.

ARLETA. Nodding isn't enough. I need your voice. Your loud voice. [*She raises her voice.*] Do you understand, priest?

ANTONIO. [*Standing in a military attention posture, with a salute.*] Yes, sir!

ARLETA. Say "yes, ma'am." I'm not a sir.

ANTONIO [*Very loudly*]. Yes, madam.

ARLETA. [*Nodding.*] Relax! And you are free to go.

Antonio starts walking toward the exit. After, couple steps, Arketta stops him.

ARKETTA. [*With great confidence.*] Wait, Antonio! Nobody comes to see the Great Arleta and returns hungry. [*She claps her hands three times.*]

Kapoza, Arketta's personal lawyer and financier, enters.

KAPOZA. Yes, ma'am.
ARKETTA. [*She gives orders.*] Use the code P C one M.
KAPOZA. [*Talking to himself but loud enough to be heard.*] Personal check of one million.

Kapoza writes a check and gives it to Antonio, who thanks him and exits.

KAPOZA. [*To Arketta.*] Anything else I can help you with, ma'am?
ARKETTA. Get ready! We are leaving.
KAPOZA. I'm ready, ma'am!
ARKETTA. Wait for me in the car.

Kapoza exits.

ARKETTA. Mom, I'm on my way to pick up my father-to-be.
ARLETA. Sure! I been expecting him today. He hasn't accepted his car gift yet?
ARKETTA. Yes, he will! Just a little good pressure will change his mind.
ARLETA. Okay. Good luck!

Arketta kisses her mother and walks toward the exit. She meets her daughter, Belgina, entering the stage, by the exit.

BELGINA. [*Contented.*] Hey, Mom! How are you doing?
ARKETTA. [*Smiling.*] You came to visit your grandma?
BELGINA. Exactly! Is she here?
ARKETTA. Sure! I'll see you when I get back. I'm rushing.
BELGINA. Okay, Mom! I love you!

They hug. Arketta exits. Belgina walks to where her grandmother is standing. She takes out from her purse all the newspaper articles about her grandmother's affair with David Jr. Arleta is cleaning her spectacles and doesn't see Belgina until she speaks.

BELGINA. [*In a high-pitched voice, excited.*] Grandma! [*She drops the newspapers on the coffee table.*]

Arleta jumps and drops her glasses. She tries to look for them. Belgina picks them up for her.

BELGINA. [*Pointing at the pile of newspapers with bitter disgust.*] Grandma! Have you been reading the news?
ARLETA. [*Calm.*] Is there any breaking news this morning?
BELGINA. [*She raises her voice, panting.*] Have you been reading the news for the last three weeks?
ARLETA. [*Looking at the newspapers, very calm.*] What's in the headlines?
BELGINA. [*Sadly.*] Arleta Yavanov and David Schumerman Jr.!
ARLETA. What about them? What strikes your nerve so badly?
BELGINA. The incident, the press, the shame—
ARLETA. Incidents or the press won't gimme an identity. I'll remain who I am and who I always am no matter what incident trips up my way. 'Cause what I am is a value from inside myself. I believe in it, and nobody'll be able to take it away from me.
BELGINA. [*Exasperated, speaking fast.*] Is everything okay with you, Grandma? Don't you feel the same shame that I'm feeling? How strange that you have distanced yourself. You used to be the pride of all Aerosanam. The big feared Arleta, the Iron Lady, the chastity billionaire. But now see how reporters are making fun of you. [*She takes a couple newspapers and shows them to Arleta.*] You can read titles like "The Aerosanam Phenomenon Lady Drops on Her Knee for a Seventeen-Year-Old Boy." [*She shuffles the newspapers.*] This other one says: "Are We Witnessing the End of the Iron Lady's Era as She Keeps Forcing a Nonworthy Boy to Marry Her?" [*She drops the newspapers back on the coffee table. She speaks sadly and slowly.*] Sincerely, Grandma! Tell me what's wrong with you! Aren't there people

of your age that you can marry? I've been living in Aerosanam for the last thirty-five years; I haven't heard about you with a man. Why only now? You waited only when I went on vacation to the Bahamas?

ARLETA. [*Indifferently.*] Is that all?

BELGINA. [*Rising.*] You want more?

ARLETA. [*Very calm.*] I know about everything you're telling me. About the press, I can exercise my will over its printings if I want too. I can tell reporters to write anything I want, and they'll obey like dogs. Now, if I let everything run its natural course, it's for one reason. I keep that reason to myself. The other reason is, naturally, if a woman is following a man, the entire world would be alerted.

BELGINA. [*Worried.*] What kind of marriage will it be that you'll be engaged with a little boy of the age of your great-grandson? Won't you be ashamed to open your legs to him? Or do you have another specific concept of marriage? People traditionally marry to start a family. But you, a seventy-year-old lady, a postmenopausal lady, how are you gonna make it?

ARLETA. First off, I am not old. I fit the definition of young. Young is whoever is between the ages of seven to seventy-seven years. Second off, I'm not past menopause. [*Belgina opens wide her mouth and eyes in surprise.*] I'm still seeing my periods. I'll be the oldest woman in the modern era to fulfill her dream. I've been constantly dreaming to get married, to have kids that I'd raise together with my hubby. [*Slight pause.*] Sarah, in the Christian Bible, was reported to have delivered her son Isaac when she was ninety-five years old or so. That was like four thousand years ago. In the modern era, I'll be the oldest woman to get pregnant at age seventy. Nothing's impossible in this world.

BELGINA. That's you. But did you calculate all the odds of being married to a seventeen-year-old boy?

ARLETA. In the last seventy years of my life, I've slept with men only three times. Beside, in the last forty years, I haven't slept with a single man. I'm just like a virgin. My seventeen-year-old husband would feel comfortable with a virgin seventy-year-old lady.

BELGINA. You really opening your mouth to tell me that? Grandma, what's wrong with you? I'm still wondering.

ARLETA. Are you through? Did you finish your negative praise? Or is there more coming from your ass?

BELGINA. There's more. [*She bursts.*] I think you need help. I'm gonna admit you to a psychiatric hospital for help.

ARLETA. Is that all?

BELGINA. [*Yelling.*] I ain't gonna allow your adventure to happen. I swear over my dead body. Do you get me?

ARLETA. Tell me when you are done.

BELGINA. I am done.

ARLETA. [*She applauds.*] Congratulation, little worm! This is the first time in my life I've received direct threats. Threats from a little pathetic gecko like you. Do you really know that beside me, you are nothing? Do you know that Aerosanam would've been a bush if I wasn't its resident? Do you know that Arleta Yavanov is the strongest woman on earth?

BELGINA. [*Normally.*] A queen doesn't say to herself that she's a queen.

ARLETA. There're Arleta-holics everywhere in Aerosanam. So don't think you'll take my queenship away from me whether I say it or not.

BELGINA. I swear that it's gonna be either me dying or your marriage. I ain't gonna let it happen. It's a shame for not only you but for all of us.

ARLETA. [*Softly.*] I understand. I got your back. Carry out your threats. You have my blessings. A hundred percent support from me.

BELGINA. Just tell me that you won't force that little boy to marry you, and everything'll be all right.

ARLETA. Before I tell you what you want, tell me if you'll be able to handle the consequences of your own acts.

BELGINA. My own acts?

ARLETA. You've been so unfaithful to your lovely husband. You've been sleeping around with almost every servant in your house. You've been giving big checks to your lovers. The vacation cruise you went on to the Bahamas was a swinger cruise. For four months, you slept with almost a thousand men on that cruise. You accuse your husband of being very jealous, and you usually play the innocent. I know every single man that you sleep with in Aerosanam. [*Sigh.*] Now listen to me. You have a beautiful family, a lovely husband and four little angels. Don't push me to destroy it.

BELGINA. [*She drops to her knees and sadly implores Arleta.*] I believe that you are the true Iron Lady. I'm gonna leave you alone. But please. Don't say a word about me to anybody.

ARLETA. That's not all. If your husband finds out about all your affairs, he'll take you to court, and he may be entitled to all your fortune. All the wealth that you inherited from me will be gone to him.

BELGINA. I have underestimated your strength. I apologize. I'm very sorry. Grandma! Please forgive me!

Belgina sobs. She stays in her kneeling position for a couple seconds or so. Then Arleta helps her stands up. They hug for a few seconds.

ARLETA. I'm gonna tell you something that you never heard before. You'll be the second one to know this secret of my life. The only other person who knows this is your mother. Are you ready?

BELGINA. [*She nods.*] It ain't gonna be scary, right?

ARLETA. [*She shakes her head.*] Not that scary. However, there're deaths involved.

BELGINA. Go ahead.

ARLETA. You haven't seen my pictures when I was a little girl, have you? I was the prettiest girl on earth. I was believed to be a reincarnation of an angel, of the Virgin Mary, or somebody along that line of beauty. I was so beautiful that even Jesus couldn't've resisted if I had to seduce him. I was extremely gorgeous! [*Pause.*] I caused trouble to many people at that time. Young and old people wanted me, and they fought a war of conquest, all just for me... God gave me a heart that didn't want men. I was so quiet and chaste, not the least impressed by any man... I never wore makeup. However, I was able beat any women who wore the highest makeup. [*Pause.*] At age fifteen, I was forced by my parents to marry a multibillionaire old man from Russia, Moisovich Yavanov, your grandfather. He was ninety-five years old. We had a ten-million-dollar wedding ceremony. Unfortunately, the night of honeymoon, the poor Moisovich after taking my virginity, died on top of me. I was so frightened. Remember, I was only fifteen. After his death, I inherited all his fortune and his empire business. I became the youngest billionaire that the world's ever witnessed... A couple weeks later, I found that I was pregnant. At age sixteen, I delivered your mother and named her Arketta Yavanov... I never was involved in any relationship whatsoever until the age of twenty-five. I was seduced by another billionaire. But he died on top of me the very first time I had sex with him... What a scary situation.... That was only the second time in my life that I'd slept with men. And both times, the men died while sharing with me. I decided that I would never sleep with a man again... My decision was not serious. But I kept it for five long years. At age thirty, I was involved in the same scenario as the two preceding. My third man died under the same circumstances. The deal was sealed for me. I came to realize that I possessed a kind of unexplained power in my female budget-- [*She points at the root of her legs.*]-- that was killing my partners. In thirty years, I swallowed it three times only, and each time my man died on top of me. I decided that I'd never sleep with a man again until when God would tell me who my true man was... the man who'd never die if I slept with him. [*Pause.*] I waited forty years, and finally, the voice of God spoke to me precisely and clearly...It said, I quote, "Your husband's name is David Schumerman. Find him in Aerosanam." [*Pause.*] I didn't know that person. Your mother looked for him and came with the boy, the only qualified person who has that name.

Belgina's cell phone rings. She looks at the screen.

BELGINA. [*In a hurried manner.*] It's my husband! I gotta go. [*She hugs Arleta.*] Enjoy your life to the fullest, please. And fulfill your dreams. I'll see you soon. I love you!

ARLETA. Well, tell your hubby to stop by later. He hasn't briefed me this week yet.

BELGINA. With pleasure. [*She stays standing, texting.*]

Arleta claps her hands. Kalol and Apolosa enters.

ARLETA. [*To Kalol.*] Wipe those chairs. They're so dusty. My husband-to-be is on his way. I don't want him to stain his clothes. [*Slight pause.*] I'll be back.

KALOL. With pleasure, ma'am!

Kalol wipes the couches. Arleta exits. Belgina walks slowly toward the exit, her attention focused on her phone, texting.

    Arketta, Kapoza and David Jr., enter. They meet with Belgina before she exits. They exchange greetings.

ARKETTA. [*To David Jr.*] Dad, this is my daughter, Belgina. [*To Belgina.*] Belgina, this is David Schumerman. Your soon-to-be grandfather.

DAVID JR. [*Shaking Belgina's hand, coldly.*] Nice to meet you.

BELGINA. Nice to meet you too, Grandpa.

DAVID JR. [*Coldly.*] I ain't your grandpa yet. I may never be. [*Delighted.*] Besides, you're the lady I saw the day before at the airport, right?

BELGINA. I didn't see you, but I was coming from a long vacation to the Bahamas.

DAVID JR. The man you grabbed by his collar is my brother-in-law. He's married to my sister, Kassandra.

BELGINA. I apologize, Grandpa. I'll invite all of your family soon to my place. I'll have to officially present my sincere apology to your brother-in-law.

DAVID JR. Don't invite us now until we settle this matter.

BELGINA. [*Smiling.*] Are you gonna marry my granny, right? [*Arketta is very contented by Belgina's question and smiles broadly.*]

DAVID JR. [*Quietly.*] Let time decide about that matter, please.

Belgina's cell phone rings. She shakes David Jr.'s hand again.

BELGINA. [*Hurriedly.*] I gotta go. My husband is waiting. Nice to meet you, Grandpa. I love you.

Belgina exits. David Jr. and Arketta walk to the living room. Arketta asks David Jr. to have a seat, and then she exits. David Jr. refuses to sit.
  Kapoza stays in the living room. Kalol is still wiping chairs. Apolosa enters. He hugs Kapoza.

KAPOZA. We work at the same place, but we don't see each other.
APOLOSA. It's kind of crazy when somebody else has to set your daily schedule, I believe so, right? Working for a boss's personal runs are just another form of slavery. You don't keep times for yourself nor for your family.
KALOL. I love it anyway.
APOLOSA. You love it 'cause you fit in the category of home slaves.
KALOL. I ain't a slave. I can't be no slave. I'm employed. Slaves don't get paid. They never been thanked. Slaves are machines. Their only salary is lashes and whips. [*She looks at him.*] I make a lot of money just for helping a rich billionaire with her daily affairs. I make easy and more money than the lady serving you alcohol at your local bar. I make more money than any Congresswoman. My boss doesn't yell at me. She never hurts me. So where's my slavery? [*Slight pause.*] I ain't no slave.
KAPOZA. [*Changing the subject.*] Eh, man, you promised me to gimme the book I asked for the next time you see Kalol. [*He points at Kalol.*] Here she is. Where's the book?
APOLOSA. [*To Kapoza.*] Just step aside for a minute, please.

Kapoza walks away and stops, looking at Apolosa as he speaks loudly to Kalol.

APOLOSA. [*To Kalol.*] Hey, man, I need your help, please. This guy here needs my book. Tell him just you have that book in your possession, but you can't give it to him, 'cause you need it now or 'cause you lost it. Okay?

KALOL. Okay.

Apolosa approaches Kapoza and tries to explain. However, Kapoza cuts him short.

KAPOZA. Why you doing this to me, man? You could just hav told me no.

APOLOSA. I don't know what you talking about.

KAPOZA. I heard your whole conversation with her. [*He points at Kalol.*] Did you realize how loud you were speaking?

APOLOSA. So?

KAPOZA. You were not supposed to play this entire scenario. When I asked you earlier, you could've just said, "Hey, man, I do have the book but I can't lend it to you."

APOLOSA. Do you forget that I been refusing to give you this book since day one? But you never understood. So I came to our colleague, and I asked her loudly to help me settle this matter. Fortunately, you heard me explaining to her.

KAPOZA. Asshole!

APOLOSA. That's a fighting offense. You know it.

KAPOZA. If you wanna fight, I'll help you put some love in your shit.

APOLOSA. Shut that freakin' mouth of yours.

KALOL. [*To Apolosa and Kapoza.*] Hey, guys! You need to respect his highness, our boss. [*She points at David Jr.*] The boss is here, but you cussing and fussing at each other with no consideration for his presence? Come on, guys. [*To David Jr.*] Boss, have a seat, please. In few days, all this will be yours. You'll be running all of Aerosanam and, consequently, all of us.

David Jr., with a shake of his head, refuses to sit. He signals Kalol to come to him. Kalol approaches him. He releases his belt and pulls his pants forward so that there is enough space to view what's inside. David Jr. points in his pants, inviting Kalol to take look. She refuses to look and runs away, smiling. David Jr. calls Apolosa and invites him to look in his pants. Apolosa looks inside David Jr.'s pants and starts laughing very loud. David Jr. does the same to Kapoza. Kapoza laughs very long and very loud.

KALOL. [*Smiling.*] What's going on?

David Jr. beckons Kalol with a hand gesture. She responds to the invitation to look inside his pants. As soon as she looks, she laughs heartily, joining Apolosa and Kapoza, still laughing. David Jr. is just standing, very quiet and serious.

KAPOZA. Lemme see again.

David Jr. shows Kapoza again. Kapoza's laughing intensity increases. Arleta enters. All the laughter ceases instantaneously. Kapoza, Apolosa, and Kalol stand straight and quiet.

ARLETA. Something going on?
KAPOZA. No.
ARLETA. You were all laughing like during a TV late-night show. What was funny?
KAPOZA. I was not laughing.
APOLOSA. I was not laughing.
KALOL. I was not laughing.
ARLETA. I was not far and I heard y'all. [*To David Jr.*] Were they laughing at you? [*David Jr. shakes his head.*] Were they laughing at all? [*David Jr. shakes his head.*] You gotta be kidding me. [*To Kapoza, Apolosa, and Kalol.*] I give orders for you to carry out. Believe me, I can turn this earth upside down if I wish to. Or I can send you skiing on a busy highway. [*Pause.*] Anyway, you can leave me alone with my man.
KALOL. Alone, ma'am?
ARLETA. Someone adjust my chair, please.

Kalol comes and adjusts her chair. Arleta nods and gives Kalol a sign to leave.
Kalol, Kapoza, and Apolosa exit. Smiling, Arleta opens her arms and invites David Jr. to approach.

ARLETA. Come here, darling! Come and taste the sweet lips of your lovely soon-to-be wife.

David Jr. doesn't move. Instead, he asks questions.

DAVID JR. What does God look like?
ARLETA. I didn't see him. I heard his voice only.
DAVID JR. What does God's voice sound like?
ARLETA. Like a human voice.
DAVID JR. A male or female?
ARLETA. I can't tell, but I guess it sounds like a childlike male voice, with a mixture of both feminine and masculine pitches.
DAVID JR. I thought God's voice will be like a roar of a lion or thunder-like voice that would tear into pieces the person who hears it.
ARLETA. Sure! God may reveal himself differently to each one of us depending on his state of acceptance. If you believe that God's voice is thunder, then it will be a thunder.
DAVID JR. I ain't really willing to hear God's voice. The idea itself is so frightening. I'm just a little nothing compared to God. Believe me, I don't wanna hear God's voice. I ain't either ready or wishing for it.
ARLETA. But you have to obey God if he sends a message to you through his humble servant, myself. A person who spent forty years requesting God to speak to her about a choice of husband.
DAVID JR. You should've recorded the voice of God to make it authentic. There's no proof for me to believe that it's truly God who spoke to you.
ARLETA. You just gotta trust me. I been living for seventy years. There've been more than a thousand men who've courted and tried to seduce me. But I've rejected them all. I wanted God to tell me my true husband.

DAVID JR. And God told you that your husband is David Schumerman, right?

ARLETA. God told me that you are my husband. I have to follow God's promise, respect it, and accomplish it at any price.

DAVID JR. If God told you that I'm your husband, tell God to tell me also that you're my future wife. I can't believe you only 'cause you claim that it's God who told you. Even if it were God, where's the proof? Tell God to write it down. Tell God to sign a petition that I'm the only superhusband for you, requested by him. Tell God to get his signature notarized. I can show him where free notary services are located, so he wouldn't have to spend a penny.

ARLETA. I gotta trust God. I'm his humble servant. I can't impose a guideline on my God. He told me what he told me, and I'll accomplish it no matter what.

DAVID JR. Tell him to talk to you while I'm with you so we can both hear his voice.

ARLETA. The opportunity to hear God's voice doesn't come twice in a lifetime. I've got some thoughts of my own on how to carry out God's instructions. God ain't gonna do for me what he already told me to do.

DAVID JR. What if it were just an autodiffusion of your own thoughts? Libraries and the Internet are packed with millions of stories about people who had a mental breakdown and schizophrenia. They've reportedly heard voices from so-called God who directed them to hurt themselves or hurt their neighbors.

ARLETA. I've got no ability of autodiffusion of my thoughts. Those who believe they are hearing voices are connected to somewhere in the twilight zone. They also hear those voices repeatedly, and they give up to subtle solicitations. [*Pause.*] I heard the voice of God only once…After forty long years of prayers… It didn't tell me to hurt anybody… It only gave me the name of my future husband, David Schumerman. In Aerosanam, there're only two Schumermans. One is already taken; the other is you. So do the math.

DAVID JR. God didn't say that your husband has to be in Aerosanam. You may try to find him around the state of Jefferson or in the US.

ARLETA. Aerosanam is my store. God won't gimme something out of my warehouse.

DAVID JR. Tell God to tell me also that I'm your husband. 'Cause there're two sides involved, God can't just tell it to you alone and hide it from me.

ARLETA.[*Rising.*] Lemme repeat to you that I don't give orders to God. I don't even speak to him. He responded to my prayers that I've been saying for more than forty years. That's all.

DAVID JR. In that case, you gotta wait forty more years before you get my answer, 'cause I gotta be asking God the same prayer you said. [*Mockingly.*] I guess he takes forty years to answer prayers, right?

ARLETA. God's already spoken, He can't speak twice for the same situation. It's my execution of his orders that matters, not your prayers. [*Pause.*] I'll tell you in the little Spanish that I know: *que viva Dios*!

DAVID JR. [*Shaking his head.*] I'm not impressed. How do you decide if you are freakin' insane? A collection of heavenly question marks?

ARLETA. At least I ain't hurting you, nor I ain't hurting myself, am I?

DAVID JR. [*Energetically.*] You hurting me. My family dynamics are undergoing depressing changes 'cause of you. If you had a chance to screen my heart and the heart of my entire family, including my girlfriend, Lynette, you'd have realized how evilly you're hurting all of us.

ARLETA. [*Sadly.*] Oh my poor baby! I ain't intending to hurt you. However— [*She looks down.*]— However— [*She looks at him and speaks slowly.*]— Love's a heavy cross-- heavier than the one that Jesus carried-- that one carries without knowing why he's hurting himself with such a load so much weightier than himself. [*She pauses, then speaks normally.*] My point is, and I heavily stand by it, I ain't going against God's will. I spent a lifetime waiting for this event. I'm gonna carry out God's choice. It may seem that I'm hurting you, but you'll realize afterward that it's carried out for your benefit.

DAVID JR. For my benefit? [*He forces a scornful smile.*] Come on, Arleta. [*He shakes his head.*] Don't think that I care about inheriting your billions. If it were so, I'd have accepted your offer the very first day. But I kept running away from you for the last three weeks. [*Pointing.*] In addition, that's not all. I'll run away from you even if it means death to me.

ARLETA. [*Applauding.*] Congratulations, fiancé! Congratulations! [*Nodding.*] I like people who challenge my power and me. Because they give me much more time to redo my calculus. [*Calmly.*] So far, you're free to go…. But, lemme warn you please… If you don't agree to willingly marry me on your own volition, I'm gonna be disastrously obligated to make you marry me against your little will.

DAVID JR. *A finale?*

ARLETA. Big pardon?

DAVID JR. So what's gonna happen afterward?

ARLETA. That, you'll have to find the answer to on your own. For my part, I'll have just accomplished God's will.

DAVID JR. [*Complaining intensely, near tears.*] I don't feel the love, Arleta. I don't feel any iota of love. Should it be this way? [*He turns slowly, making a circle, speaking sadly.*] I was expecting to be filled by the vibes of love from you to me. But so far I only feel threats and death around me… It seems like God is inciting you to destroy my little world and my birthright to free will. [*Looking at her steadily.*] There's no love coming out of your mouth nor from anywhere around your place. [*Recoiling.*] I feel scared.

ARLETA. [*Not the least impressed.*] The secret of love isn't about receiving or feeling it. The secret of love lays in giving it. [*Sighs.*] Then and only then, you'll feel it around you. [*Sighs.*] The feeling of threat, fear, and death around here, as you claim it, is coming from inside of you. Those emotions are just reflections of your own world inside you. [*Sighs.*] If you change from within and replace fear with love, you'll feel love from my mouth and around me. [*Softly.*] Give it first, then feel it back, please.

DAVID JR. [*Rising.*] I can't give love to a person who's coercing me to love her. 'Cause that's ego, not love.

ARLETA. [*Calmly.*] It's not ego. What's your frame of reference? The tongue can't tell the degree of love I carry for you.

DAVID JR. [*Normally.*] I'm just curious. [*Pause.*] Have ever asked yourself why are most human predators, parasites, dependents like gigantic mosquitoes in Aerosanam backing you up? They adore you instead of hurting you... Do you know why? [*Silence.*] Well, I'll tell you the reason. 'Cause that's what you do every day. Do you know what you do daily? [*Silence.*] People bow at your every word 'cause you inspire fear, not love. It's your ego at work all around this city. You call it love; I call it ego. It ain't gonna work with me.

ARLETA. When dealing with me, many've told me the same thing in the past. They only underestimated my strength. My true strength is love, not ego. Not even power. So far, I've only been using one percent of my strength. So may God bless you?

DAVID JR. [*Energetically.*] You, tell God to bless you! Tell him really to bless you to the thousand fold... You claim that you speak to him, right? Tell him to take away from you that idea of marrying me. It's so awkward. It's so scary. I can't even believe that this is happening.

ARLETA. I understand your point, David. And I wish you could understand me too. I probably have a different concept of life than you do. I know that a human being is all about conflict. Conflict within himself, and conflict between himself and his family, between himself and society, and conflict between himself and the world. [*Sigh.*] If a person runs away from any conflict, or if he lacks the energy to face conflicts, then he decides to ride on a fast roller coaster that'll precipitate him to his own destruction... I have a little advice for you: do not to run away from your problems. Face them, overcome them. That'll make you a real man.

DAVID JR. [*He turns his back to her, walks couple steps, then turn around to face her again.*] I just ain't ready for all this, Arleta. I'm still a teenage boy who's still looking for himself.

ARLETA. That's true. You are still looking for yourself. However, in your search to look for yourself, you crossed a one-way line where you are not supposed to go back. You're worthy to marry the Iron Lady.

DAVID JR. [*Objecting vehemently.*] I don't feel so. I wish I could be like Jesus, but I've got no cross to carry yet.

ARLETA. Relax, David, I'll help you. Marriage's all about helping your partner. I'm the most powerful woman. And love's the sole magic wand of my power... Be calm, I'll help you.

DAVID JR. [*Mockingly.*] If you think that you're the most powerful woman on earth, why don't you marry yourself? It'll make sense to you. Forcing a defenseless boy to marry you validates and vouches for your weakness.

ARLETA. I was married to myself for forty years. All was just a preparation for your arrival in my life. Don't be scared. It's your turn now. I'm gonna offer myself as a gift to you. I'll be ready to follow your lead. [*She opens her arms.*] I'm not a lover, but I know how to say, "I love you." Come here, baby. I'm all yours. [*She takes couple steps forward.*]

DAVID JR. [*He ignores her and steps backward.*] What about Dr. Pink?

ARLETA. [*Startled.*] That's a horrible freaking name. Dr. Pink? It sounds like a porn stage name.

DAVID JR. Have you ever asked yourself why such a thing like husbands dying on top of you has been recurring?

ARLETA. Because God, my God, was preparing only you to be mine. Nobody else.

DAVID JR. I'm scared to be the next victim dying on top of you. It sounds like your big pink kills.

ARLETA. [*She laughs.*] Ha ha ha! I see now: Dr. Pink, big pink! That's how you call my "doctor big"? [*She makes an air quote with major fingers and indexes of both hands when she says the words "doctor big."*]

DAVID JR. Yeah, what about your big pink? As your husband, I'm gonna be tempted to get in, right?

ARLETA. [*Frowns.*] Why not? It's gonna be a gift to you. Do whatever you wish to do with it—even know.

DAVID JR. [*Shaking his head.*] It's so disgusting. [*Frowns.*] Big pink of old women smells like rotten tomatoes.

ARLETA. I'm like a virgin. I'm not an old lady.

DAVID JR. Even if you may fit into the virginity category, still your old pink flower is gonna smell differently. I was told that it may smell like a toxic waste.

ARLETA. Don't be fooled by people's stories. Listen to every day. Adapt to reality, because that's the highest virtue to stick to. [*She adjusts herself and opens her arms.*] Come here, I'm all yours. [*She advances toward him but stops when he walks backward to avoid her. He stops when she stops.*]

David Jr. hesitates for couple seconds. Arleta insists.

ARLETA. Don't be shy, hubby. Come here. Aren't you proud to taste the sweet lips of the most powerful woman in Aerosanam? I'm gonna warm you up as you never been warmed before.

David Jr. advances. He finally hugs Arleta, who kisses him on his lips. She grips her arms around his back.

ARLETA. [*Smiling.*] You see! It's that simple. You don't really need foreign currency to kiss a woman who loves you. [*She kisses him again.*] I live by strong mottos. But I'll easily subscribe to your lifestyle as fast and easily as I can.

DAVID JR. Is that a joke or a dream?

ARLETA. Dream! [*Smiling.*] I'm of the mission to become the oldest woman to fulfill the warmest and dearest dream of her life... I'm so driven... Thank you for all this. [*Very contented.*] I'm at the top of my life.

DAVID JR. [*Sadly*]. Unfortunately, I feel the opposite. I'm at the bottom of mine.

David Jr. adjusts himself and takes Arleta's spectacles off her face. He shakes himself off, releases himself from Arleta's grip, and runs away toward the exit. When he gets farther away, he stops and looks back at Arleta, who has been standing still, with no reaction.

DAVID JR. You're old like the Egyptian pyramids. I told you that your power to coerce me to marry you won't work. Starting today, you'll never see me again. Never again and forever.

David Jr. drops Arleta's glasses on the floor and tramples them.

DAVID JR. This is the symbol of me crushing forever your demonic dominance power over me. Enjoy the rest of your reign with those who enjoy being dominated by you, not me.

David Jr. exits. Arketta enters.

ARKETTA. [*Concerned.*] Do you want him back, Mom?
ARLETA. [*Very composed.*] Tomorrow! Let him go for now. He's gonna hide, and when he gets caught, maybe he'll change his mind.
ARKETTA. Are you sure, Mom? I can have him back in a second if you want.
ARLETA. Don't worry about him, now. I believe he's acting like a dog. Often we find that when a dog has a cord on his neck, he struggles to get away. However, when you take the cord away, he goes nowhere but sticks around.
ARKETTA. [*Nodding.*] Okay, Mon. [*Slight pause.*] Anything else I can help you with, please?
ARLETA. Tell the girls to bring my tea.
ARKETTA. With pleasure, Mom!

Arleta goes to take her seat. Arketta walks toward the exit.

Curtain.

Act 2

SCENE I

This scene is a dream. The first part happens in hell.

Curtain opens.

There are three human entities (two males and one female) seated on the floor. They are dressed in rags. They are rubbing constantly their chests and hands, and warming themselves around a small kindled fire. A couple seconds later, David Jr. enters. He is wearing ragged shorts, a T-shirt, and a tie. His arms are crossed in front of his chest, and he is rubbing his biceps to warm himself up. It is very cold, shivering. He stops a couple feet before he gets to the little group. He addresses the group. All entities speak with hoarse voices.

DAVID JR. Eh, guys! It's freezing up here more than in a refrigerated storage area. Where are we at, guys?

ENTITY 1. You are in hell. Ha ha ha! [*All three entities laugh heartily.*]

DAVID JR. [*He waits until the laughter settles.*] You stupid demons! Who told you that it's freezing in hell?

ENTITY 2. You landed in the South Pole area of hell. It gets colder here than you think. Ha ha ha!

ENTITY 3. This is still nothing yet. It is just a friendly welcome to you. The longer you stay, the more freezing it gets. Ha ha ha! [*All three entities join the laughter.*]

DAVID JR. [*Frightened.*] Noooo! I wanna get out of here. I'm not a hell citizen.

ENTITY 1. You look funny, you talk funny, and you are wearing a new and clean tie with rags. Ha ha ha!

ENTITY 2. That's the same way hell citizens wear their clothes. That's the same way hell citizens look and talk funny. Ha ha ha!

ENTITY 3. So welcome to hell, and enjoy your new citizenship. Ha ha ha! [*All three entities join the laughter.*]

DAVID JR. [*Screaming.*] Stoooop, pleeeease! You are freaking scaring me up!

David Jr. tries to run, but his steps are stalled. The three entities laugh intensely. They are even hitting their hands on the floor because they are laughing so hard.

DAVID JR. [*Serious.*] Don't laugh. It's not funny. Just help me to get out of here. I don't belong here.

Those words just fuel more laughter from the three entities. David Jr. keeps trying to flee. But he stays in the same place.

ENTITY 1. The Red Queen theory applies here. Ah ah ah!
ENTITY 2. Have you ever heard about the Red Queen theory? Ah ah ah!
ENTITY 3. The faster you run, the more you stay in the same place. Ah ah ah!

David Jr. stops running. He tries to regain his composure, but it is very cold.

DAVID JR. Can I at least join you around the fire, please?
ENTITY 1 [*Seriously.*] I would not advise you, unless you decide to stay here forever.
ENTITY 2. [*Seriously.*] Use who you are to get out of here.
ENTITY 3. [*Seriously.*] The fresher you are, the higher you can make it. Otherwise, welcome to your new eternal residence.
ENTITY 1. The more you stay here, the faster you fall in love with this place.
ENTITY 2. Once you fall in love with this place, you will never want to go back to earth.
DAVID JR. How did I land here, anyway?
ENTITY 3. You attracted hell to yourself. Ah ah ah! When you only speak about it, when your tongue is filled with the words "evil" and "devil," and when you think that your life is hell, then you are buying your hell identity, and you will go to hell. Ah ah ah!
DAVID JR. [*More frightened. He raises his arms and looks up. He bellows in rage.*] Aie!

Bunikenike, an entity wearing a white tunic enters. He stops in from of David Jr. He gives him a long mantle. David Jr. puts it around his shoulders.

BUNIKENIKE. [*With a deep-toned, calm, and bass voice.*] Relax, David! Relax. Running from hell will just make things worse than you think. It has a backward effect. The more you try to get away, the more you grow roots that will hold you deeper into hell's soil. So relax!

DAVID JR. Who are you?

BUNIKENIKE. I will tell you later.

DAVID JR. How did you find me?

BUNIKENIKE. You called me.

DAVID JR. [*Pointing at the tree entities.*] Who are those three guys up there?

BUNIKENIKE. They are just negative parts of yourself. The negatively charged parts of each person work as trampolines to propel him beyond his own limitations and troubles.

DAVID JR. Who are you?

BUNIKENIKE. Don't get distracted by trying to know who I am. It is a waste of time. It will cost you an opportunity to free yourself from your own little hell world.

DAVID JR. Is this my world?

BUNIKENIKE. You created it.

DAVID JR. I don't wanna be part of it.

BUNIKENIKE. Then who is holding you back? Who is your jailer?

DAVID JR. I don't know. Do you know?

BUNIKENIKE. Yourself. [*David Jr. points at his own chest, wondering.*] Get out of here first, then keep on with your life.

DAVID JR. How?

BUNIKENIKE. Just close your eyes, and imagine that you are out of here.

DAVID JR. [*After couple tries.*] I'm still here.

BUNIKENIKE. Where?

DAVID JR. In hell.

BUNIKENIKE. [*Yelling.*] You are hurting yourself. Do not think that you are in hell anymore. Tell me somewhere else.

DAVID JR. Where else?

BUNIKENIKE. First, imagine that you are not in hell anymore. Then, in your imagination, find a new place where you believe you want to be. Finally, put emotions in the images and places you are creating in your mind. Feel the images in yourself.

The scene changes. The three entities stand and exit. It is still a dream. In a single line, David Jr.'s relatives enter. They stand couple feet away from him, couple feet away from each other. They are looking at the audience. Finally, enter Arleta in a wedding dress. Arketta is behind her. They stand perpendicular to the audience, as to face David Jr. from the opposite side of the stage. From part of the stage (where David Jr. is standing) to the other side of the stage (where Arleta is now standing) stand Linzi, Lynnette, Kassandra, Andricoco, Jevus, Iberkonta, and David Sr.
    David Jr. is shocked. He looks at Bunikenike with big eyes.

DAVID JR. I din't wanna be here. I wanted to be somewhere in a paradise room with my girlfriend, Lynnette. I din't wanna be on earth, standing for a wedding ceremony with this ugly old woman of Arleta.

BUNIKENIKE. Your life today is the result of what you have created in the past. You need to face it. Nobody else will do it for you.

The three entities renter the stage. They bring shoes, a shirt, pants, a bow tie, and a tuxedo. They help David Jr. to put on his wedding getup.

DAVID JR. [*Fearful.*] Is this happening?

BUNIKENIKE. Dreams are real. Learn to solve your problems in your dreams, and you will have less trouble in your daily life.

DAVID JR. I don't know how. [*Sigh.*] Also, I know there are dreams that can't be dreamed ever during our sleep.

BUNIKENIKE. Nothing is greater than your sleep. If you borrow it, you have to repay it back quickly.

DAVID JR. What's that mean?

BUNIKENIKE. What's that mean? I am glad that you asked. Any of your decisions has severe ramifications on those around you. You may have less trouble if you can solve your problem in your dream. [*David Jr. wants to say something, but Bunikenike points him toward the group waiting for him.*] Don't waste your time. You have to do this now, or it will do you.

DAVID JR. [*Relieved, he sighs.*] Are you my best man? I can't walk by myself. My feet are numb. It feels like I don't have any feet at all. Please be behind me.

BUNIKENIKE. [*Patting David Jr.'s shoulder.*] Good luck! [*He start walking toward the exit.*]

DAVID JR. Can I ask you for a favor before you go, please?

BUNIKENIKE. Go ahead!

DAVID JR. I still don't understand this adventure. I'm gonna repeat the question I asked earlier. Why am I here? In my imagination, I created paradise. I wanted to get to paradise along with my lovely girlfriend, Lynnette.

BUNIKENIKE. You are here because it is your burden. You can't go to paradise carrying a burden on your back. The first step to walk toward the land of paradise consists of facing all that you have created in your life; conquer it and get rid of it before you can purely create and succeed at finding yourself in paradise. [*Sigh.*] Nevertheless, it is easy to go with your loads to hell, because that's where you can burn them up and get yourself purified.

DAVID JR. I got another question that's been lingering in my mind for the last three weeks.

BUNIKENIKE. Go ahead.

DAVID JR. Does God talk to humans?

BUNIKENIKE God doesn't have a voice like that of humans. Even if he had to speak, his voice would have high vibrations and would not be heard. Animals speak too. But the pitches and vibrations of their language are too low for humans to hear.

DAVID JR. There exist up there humans who claim to hear God speaking.

BUNIKENIKE. There are entities who work for God and for the benefice of the humanity. A person may have a special connection with one of those entities, and he may hear them talking to him.

DAVID JR. What do you mean by "entity"?

BUNIKENIKE. You may call the entities as guardian angels, avatars, masters, spirits, jinn, or any name that you feel comfortable calling them. [*Sigh.*] Let me repeat what I told you early: some of those entities work with humans that are in tune with them and talk to them.

DAVID JR. Are you one of them?

BUNIKENIKE. [*Ignoring David Jr.'s question.*] Now I have to go. You have to face your problems, because you created them and you have to deal with them alone, with the influence and support of your loved ones. [*He pats David Jr. on the back.*]

DAVID JR. Why do I need help from my loved ones in general and my family in particular?

BUNIKENIKE. It is really telling you inside yourself. You are superconnected to your family in many ways. You have been sinning together for so long, and all the weight of your negative loads has been shared together. All members are integrated. Never isolated. Even if one thinks to cut off a relationship with a member of his family, the true link that bonds him to his family member will be still hardworking. [*Breath.*] The artist's rendition of family would be images of each individual carrying all members of his family on his back, himself being carried by all his loved ones. [*Sighs.*] There is a cross carried together for those who love each other in order to alleviate the loads of doom.

DAVID JR. Oh My God!

BUNIKENIKE. Oh Your God, what?

DAVID JR [*Sadly, near tears*]. I keep wondering if life has something new in store for humanity. I'm tired of listening to the same thing over and over again. Can life offer to us something new? Something beyond war, beyond love, beyond politics, religion, science, eating, sex, marriage, families, sleeping, dreaming, and all that we have? I'm tired of all this. Can life give us another order of living?

BUNIKENIKE. [*Always calm, deeply, and slowly speaking.*] You are over-thinking. You are thinking beyond your nose. Keep life simple. Enjoy what you have, and be grateful for the breath coming out of your lungs. If you want more from life, the day it will come to you, you will need something new. All humans are eternally unsatisfied. [*He tries to leave.*]

DAVID JR. [*Pleading.*] Eh! Eh! Wait, please! Before you go, I need a specific answer in order to decide on my next step about my so-called bride waiting for me on the other side. [*He points at Arleta, waiting for him.*] Did God really talk to her about me?

BUNIKENIKE. It only works when you believe it. If you believe that God will talk to you, and you keep it constantly in your mind, eventually, it is going to happen. However, that's only what I think. Everybody experiences God in his own understanding. God is so subtle and so subjective that nobody can claim to understand the ways he works... I can't really answer that question for your bride.

DAVID JR. I feel like she's a great obstacle for my happiness and my life in general.

BUNIKENIKE. Some do have a longer road to travel, but the destination is the same—success! I'm sure you will find yours in this particular goal and many others. My last words are, be your own mirror

DAVID JR. Is there any easier way to say it?

BUNIKENIKE. To be your own mirror is to see your own answer for a situation. [*He pats David Jr.'s back.*] Good luck!

Bunikenike and the three entities walk away. David Jr. turns around to look at them as they exit. Then he adjusts his tuxedo and his bow tie. He walks down the line of family members and stops a couple feet away from each one.

Linzi is his first stop.

LINZI. [*Very confident.*] David, my dear son! Life is a dream full of reality. Big things happen to those who dream big... David, your mother loves you. Be confident that everything'll be all right. [*Sighs.*] When I conceived you and gave you as a gift to this world, my dreams were to make you the most successful human that the world has never witnessed. I understand that I'm guilty for putting you in this whole situation. However, I can't rule myself out of action. Often, the heart remains quiet when the body pays the consequences of its desire. [*Sigh.*] I can't currently discuss blame and guilt. I know that you'll walk away from this biggest challenge of your life more successful than ever before. I know that time is winding down for all of us. But hang on, don't be afraid. Mommy ain't gonna let up. Mommy got your back, and Mommy's always with you... A woman is good as her word... You inherited from me all your personality. One thing that you'll never forget is Mommy will always love you! Am I clear to you? [*Silence.*] And Mommy will be continually writing sparkling emotional checks for your consideration. That's extremely important. Good luck, and may God help you!

David Jr. continues to walk silently. He stops before Lynnette.

LYNNETTE. [*Sobbing.*] Baby, you sure ya wanna do dis? Please, you ain't gon do it, are you? [*Sobs.*] Remember, I lost ma virginity to ya, an' we promised to live together until death... You ain't gon wipe out my past devotion to ya like an ocean wipes out de imprint of a ferry. Please help me find ma way in life, and I'll help ya keep yo promises. [*Sighs.*] Ma mouth is so dry. All the saliva in ma mouth is held hostage. [*She touches her chest.*] Ma heart's scramblin'. I'm cardiovascularily attacked. [*Sob.*] We both gonna suffer 'cause I'm yo heart. [*Sighs.*] The future ain't tomorrow, nor de next week, neither de next month. Somethin' ya wanna remember, our future is now. You ain't finna jump on a grenade today, hopin' to fix stuffs tomorrow. [*Deep breath.*] I been cryin' and askin' God to save our relationship. Don't give up yet, 'cause there's a gush of hope that's consistently crossin' ma heart and lightin' a very bright future for ya an' me. I loved ya, I love ya, an' I'll always love ya. [*Slight pause.*] Forever! [*As David Jr. leaves, Lynnette stretches out her hand to try to hold him. But she misses him and she stays at the same place.*]

Up There to Step

With no word, David Jr. walks past Lynnette. He stops before Kassandra.

KASSANDRA. Brother! It's summer, but it's gonna rain just on top of you. Don't worry. My hands are empty and ready to shield you up. [Pause.] Heavy rain is coming against you. I'll help you the same way I watched you struggling when you were taking your first steps. [*Pause.*] Life's putting you on the steps again where now you have to suit up... You know I gotta help you though, don't you? You know our DNA derives from the same source, right? Together, we'll touch down and win the game you're creating against yourself. [*Pause.*] I don't think you marryin' that old lady for love. It's just an unfortunate fate called luck... But don't worry. I'll help you. I love you...You know.

You can do so many impossible things with love... Today's the foundation of what tomorrow shall be. [*Sigh.*] You know I'm lookin' for words to describe your attitude. You look so worried. I believe that you're shooting yourself in your own foot. I gotta help you, though. If you cry, I'll cry with you. But I know a man ain't supposed to cry. I've witnessed that reality along my way. A man ain't supposed to have pity for his life. Otherwise, life'll take advantage of his weakness... Life's a war, and I'll fight along your side... I also believe that whether you choose Arleta or Zibo, life'll bring to you events that you need for the sake of love. I mean that life'll make your heart worthy and able to love more. Believe me, you'll make it with or without a noose on your neck. [*Deep breath.*] You're worried that you're a victim of fate, right? Life won't give you something that's greater than your ability to handle it. If life tests you, it means that you can sustain it. [*Pause.*] Many times, because of the nature of the exposure, a true man gotta act beyond his normal capacities. You know, don't just entertain delusions like Don Quixote, who was well intentioned but he ended up fighting the windmill. [*Pause.*] I'll give you some advice: be ahead of life; don't be behind it... You know, life isn't only about pork and beans. Sometimes you may walk and find nothing more than hot wires to make nooses for yourself. [*Pause.*] We didn't invent life, but we embrace it with love and the knowledge that life is a treasure... Take your life together. Life belongs to the adventuresome. [*Deep breath.*] The heart doesn't swim in isolated ocean of love. Its share its territoriality with compatible hearts. If I were you, I would've chosen both Arleta and Zibo. Life would be fun to taste between two lovers. They both love you. [*Pause.*] You need to make your choice. There's a chicken and a chicken. Arleta is a chicken, and Zibo is a chicken as well. Which one do you pick? I don't care if you work it out before you choose. However, one chicken is a giant screwdriver with the ability to open sealed doors and unlimited opportunities, and the other chicken is just a regular one. Which one do you pick? When you strip away all the differences, it turns out that you're hurting yourself for nothing. All women are just the same. All women were created equal.

Like a military commander, David Jr. quietly continues his little troop review. Next stop: his uncle Andricoco.

ANDRICOCO. Somebody alone is always in trouble. However, you are not alone. This is an event that none of your billion cells will ever forget. Adjust your attitude, and you'll dominate your destiny. You need to digest those words of wisdom. They gonna open a window to many opportunities in your life. Do the math that won't allow you to cross a line. It's your call. My role is a supporting one... So get your wish answered by your uncle. [*Slight pause.*] In many cultures, an uncle is a cornerstone and a pillar for his nieces and nephews. An uncle is at the pinnacle of every family. An uncle is a panacea. An uncle is a reference. An uncle is physically, emotionally, and mentally invested in the life of his nephews. Your mother and your entire family moved to Aerosanam to save your ass from Lynnette, who was be-lieved not to be your best match because of her race. Your mother followed me here. Unfortunately, things turned out to be worse, and Lynnette was the wanted evil. She's here to save you from the worst old woman a boy can ever have as a partner. Marrying Arleta is a complete, tremendous denial. That's what I call a nasty wedding. I swear that I'll make your marriage with Arleta fail. [*Pause.*] Arleta's negativity has got to the boiling point. I promise that you'll marry Lynnette. I'm challenging Arleta. [*Chuckles.*] It sounds like a mouse challenging an elephant. [*Seriously.*] What I can play greater than Arleta is my ability to plan and play diversion. I'll put down the greatest I can. I'm the angel of mind games. I can do better than her because I'm an unlimited edition of myself. If I don't succeed in marrying you to Lynnette, this'll be the end of all the uncles in the world. The world will dissect all remaining uncles in its core.

Silently, David Jr. passes Andricoco. He advances to Jevus.

JEVUS. [*Energetically, using all kind of hands and body gestures.*] Jou are a lucky man! If I were jou, I would never hesitate. Marrying a multibijion-aire woman? Come on, boy! She said God has chosen jou among a bijion men. How lucky you are! [*Pause.*] Do jou wanna run away? Why? Luck does not come twice... That old lady Arleta, she will be dying soon. Jou will keep all her money with jou once she is gone. Den jou will return to jour girlfriend, Lynnette Zibo... Just wake up. Jou are acting as if you were in a dream. [*Pause.*] Dis is jour unique chance of a lifetime. Dis wealth and good life come with bijions in money, power, and de ability to help. Jou will be rich like a garbage. Rats and many rodents added to bijions of other insects like worms will come to jou for jour abundance. [*Pause.*] Tink about Einstein, Jesus, Mozart, and many others. All their sermons, music, notes, theories have just one thing in common. Dey help us take a step forward toward a new level of humanity.

Take jour love for Lynnette as the sun. If it disappears tonight, to-morrow it will come back. *Pero* after de dark nights of jour life dat jou will spend with the Iron Lady Arleta, jou will raise stronger dan any man dat has ever existed, and jou will return to offer jour life back to jour sun, Lynnette. [*Sighs.*] She may not even be aware of what happened. [*Sighs.*] Do not let dis chance go away.... Go ahead and eat de holy forbidden fruit. It is so delicious. *Tu sabe lo que esto ablando?* [*Silence.*]

Dere are pawnshops and credit unions. De first is a mini convenient store, and de other is a bank. Do jou know what dey have in common? Dey serve people de same way jour fiancée, de richest woman in Aerosanam, has been serving everybody around here. Jou have to get to dose places or call if jou need financial services. *Pero* jou have been chosen not to go to neither to a pawnshop nor to a bank. Jour service is so unique. It is a self-shipped big cat with bijions of shining green pubic hairs. Green dat can dry de underwater and turn it into a living paradise for humans.

Dis is the time jou have to be away from de favorite greediness called love. Take de money first, and love will follow. Money is de firstborn on earth. De second fatty daughter of earth is called woman. Dey both are faxed to men after a long call and after years of hard labor. In jour case, money and woman are autofaxing and autoshipping demselves to jou. Jou are holding jourself under de belt. Is it because jou are afraid to be a man, right? [*Sighs.*] Look how cowardly jou are, missing jour unique loud singing chance. Come on, boy, wake up!

Jou want to play de hero of love for Lynnette? It is more disgraceful. Romeo and Juliet, Isolde and Tristan, and many other love stories are fake. Dey are just products of the rich imagination of deir authors. A martyr for love does not sound real. A man does not care about his heart. He cares about his pocket. A man cares about how much money he has in his bank account. Jou have been solicited to freely put a gigantic amount of cash in jour account, and jou are declining de offer. Come on! Come on, broder-in-law.

Silently, David Jr. advances to his next stop, Iberkonta.

IBERKONTA. Everythin' happens for a reason. You better ask yo'self why this ain't happenin' to anybody else but you. You done think you gettin' raped, don't you? If so, just be strong 'bout it. Stop moanin' like a toddler. At seventeen, you already old enough to be a man. [*Sigh.*] If I were you, I'd probably give it a bite, marry that old fatigued carapace, and see what'll be the next menu on the table of life. You won't regret it, because the choices we done made in life have a reversible process. It ain't never too late to return to yo initial point. Even if you done thinking that it's late, there be choices and necessary lessons to learn from that point...Ain't nothing wrong about tryin' [*Sigh.*] Life's a kind of donut that you done constantly making, and it gets better as one goes along. The more you fail, the better you become. [*Pause.*] Ain't nobody created to regress but to progress. [*Sigh.*] I want you to learn all and nothing at the same time. I want yo to benefit all and none at the same time. There ain't no accident; there ain't no injustice either. What done happening to you now is the result of many of yo own makings. I hope you done heard that before, din't you? [*Breath.*] I believe that life is done putting everybody in the right place and at the right time. Life is like energy. Energy ain't created or destroyed. Energy is only transformed. Likewise, in life, ain't nothing is created anymore. There's only transformation and recycling of the same matter, energy, air, and fire.

Life ain't gonna walk behind yo back and stab you. It ain't gonna walk before you to show you yo' way. Life may walk alongside with you as a silent observer. [*Sigh.*] If you done messing with life, you get rewarded, not by life but by yo'self. For that reason, I urge you to make yo life easier and simpler. If you done making it difficult or if you be thinking that you a victim, it means that ain't learned nothing yet.

I ain't gonna ask you to like money nor love. I ain't never want you to worry about left or right, between Arleta and Lynnette. I want you to stay in the middle and wait for the tides of life to push you where you truly belong. [*Pause.*] Swimming against the tides of life may be hard for you to sustain. It may cause you unnecessary effort, unneeded exhaustion, and tremendous consequences. [*Pause.*] Life done known why it done put you at this point in yo life where you gotta undergo all this struggle. Either you created it, or if it be a belief you borrowed from yo'self, from yo mother or yo aunt, all you done need to do is fight back. Ain't no need to give up, but when all yo strength currency is spent, step aside and watch, relax, and observe yo life. Recharge and fight back. Ain't no need to just adopt an extreme point. Fluctuate, give up, fight, and give to God what you believe to be beyond yo capacities. Life is an eternal war.

You done working against gravity. Just go about yo life, and if you be strong enough, the law of evolution gotta reward you with a survivor trophy. To survive, you need to evolve. To evolve, you need to see changes around you and adapt. This Arleta is helping you to evolve, to take one more step on the ladder of life. Yo sole responsibility is that you are the troubleshooter. You give it to life, and life gives it back to you, like an echo. Making a decision always carries many responsibilities. If you do something wrong, you and only you be accountable.

The final stop before David Jr. gets to his bride is David Sr.

DAVID SR. Who in life wanna be a mediocre person? Who does put self-degrade or death in his agenda? You may sometimes find me looking for my shoes. Please note, it helps me fulfill my contract to myself. After saying this, I know that there are many procrastinations. The financial pie has to be seen shrinking and being crushed by the power of love. Love is more powerful than death. Death is more powerful than power, and power is more powerful than money. The deduction is yours to draw. The call is yours to make with consideration of the benefit-to-cost ratio. [*Sigh.*] Do what you love; sometimes it has costs to pay. [*Slight pause.*] I don't want you to be involved in something bigger than yourself. I'm totally opposed to all this Arleta's business. But I'm gonna turn it over to the hands of God. God works in a manner that'd never be understood by men. If it's the will of God, may it be accomplished! Good luck.

David Jr. continues past David Sr. He now walks in slow motion to Arleta, who opens her arms wide to welcome him. Meanwhile, Linzi has been struggling to move. She finally does so. She walks behind everybody and, as David Jr. approaches Arleta, interposes herself between the two. She stops David Jr.

LINZI. [*Commanding.*] I'll never let you marry this old lady, who is the same age as my grandmother. [*Calling.*] Lynnette! Lynnette!

Lynnette rushes to where Linzi is standing. Linzi takes Lynnette's and David Jr.'s hands, puts them together, and shows them the exit. David Jr. and Lynette walk toward the stage left exit. Linzi whistles. Andricoco picks up a gun from the floor. He walks past Arleta. Then, walking backward, he covers the couple as they walk toward the exit. Everybody is looking steadily at them (David Jr., Lynnette, and Andricoco) as they exit.

Linzi sighs. She was standing in front of Arleta. She turns ninety degrees and stands perpendicular to Arleta. She makes gestures with her hand, raising her elbow up as if she wants to strike her from her right side, diagonally. Arleta doesn't move. Linzi walks away. Arleta looks behind her toward Arketta, who nods.

ARKETTA. [*Very calm.*] Nobody toys with the almighty Arleta... Linzi's rough courage will hurt her butt harder than she thinks. [*Pause.*] Sooner or later, she'll be crawling again like a baby. She won't have anybody else to blame than herself.

Curtain.

SCENE 2
In a bedroom. There is a bed, where David Jr. and Lynnette are sleeping.
David Jr.

DAVID JR. [*He wakes up and sits up, panting heavily, one hand on his chest.*]
Aaaaaahhhh!
LYNNETTE. [*She sits up too, holds David Jr., and cries out.*] Aaaaaahhhh!
DAVID JR. [*Holding her tight.*] What's wrong, baby? What's wrong?
LYNNETTE. I heard ya screamin', then I screamed the same way. What's
wrong?
DAVID JR. [*Sighing.*] I just dreamed that I was in hell.
LYNNETTE. You're in hell? That's scary; that a freakin' nightmare.
DAVID JR. I was a visitor to hell. Fortunately, it was just a short visit. Now
I understand why they call it hell.
LYNNETTE. [*Softly.*]. Relax! It just a dream.
DAVID JR. No, this one was so clear. It was not a dream. It was so clear. I
was in hell, then in a wedding ceremony…In a second dream, I was walking
like a lamb being led to a slaughterhouse, with triumph and honor. Then I
woke up in this room. [*He looks around, preoccupied.*] The dream continued.
Four people were in this room, two women and two men. They tied me
up, and they took me with them. The women talked to you and asked for
your cooperation; otherwise, you'd make things worse. You stayed here,
in this den, and you didn't call neither my family nor the police. The next
morning, you returned to my family's place and kept my kidnapping adventure secret.
LYNETTE.[*Coddling.*] Chill out, baby! Ain't nothing gon happen to ya.

They calm down and lie down. From underneath the bed, Kapoza, Apolosa, and
Kalol come out. David Jr. and Lynnette are baffled and stay silent for a short
while..

KALOL. [*Mocking.*] Where you think you are hiding? That's where we
sleep, babe!

APOLOSA. Where you think you are hiding? That's where we live.

KAPOZA. You are lucky and stupid, boy. Nobody on earth can make billions of dollars the easy way like you. You are running away from wealth? Come on!

APOLOSA. You are on the loose, boy. You look like a crazy boy trying to run in the expressway along with high-speed cars.

KALOL. Chairs and beds know how to play games. You gotta know where you getting yourself.

After the moment of surprise, David Jr. and Lynnette look at each other, then get precipitously out of their bed and try to escape. They are immediately brought under control. Apolosa holds David Jr., with his two hand behind his back. Likewise, Kalol is holding Lynnette.

KAPOZA. [*Standing in front of David Jr.*] David! We can do it the easy or the hard way. Which one do you choose?

DAVID JR. [*Furious.*] Go to hell.

KAPOZA. [*Slapping David Jr.*] If you don't wanna cooperate, in the next few minutes, your face may not be recognized even by your wretch girlfriend.

DAVID JR. [*Irritably.*] I'll make you eat your own shit... I promise.

KAPOZA. [*Slapping David Jr.*] You bleeding already? That was fast.

DAVID JR. [*Struggling to release himself from Apolosa's grip.*] I swear that I'll kill y'all.

KAPOZA. Kill us or not, we don't care. We need just you to follow what we gonna ask. And everything'll go smoothly. If you resist, we do have an official permit to use extreme and excessive force, if necessary.

KALOL [*To David Jr.*]. You were showing us last time inside your pants. It looked that you din't any penis at all... So what did you stick inside that little ugly girlfriend of yours?

Lynnette struggles and temporarily releases herself from Kalol's grip. She tries to attack Kapoza and Apolosa. But she is brought straight back under Kalol's control. David Jr. is struggling to help Lynnette.

DAVID JR. [*Screaming at Kalol.*] Eh, don't hurt her. She's innocent.

KALOL. I've got no intent to harm your girlfriend. However, if you don't cooperate, I'll use her as a bait against you.

DAVID JR. [*Calming down.*] Okay! Let's make a deal. If I agree to go with you, are you gonna let Lynnette go?

KALOL. Absolutely! We got no order to bring her with us. Nevertheless, we can take her with you if necessary.

DAVID JR. I give up. I'm gonna go with you. But let her go, please.

KALOL. Tell her not to strike back. She'll hurt herself.

DAVID JR. [*To Lynnette.*] Baby, don't fight back, please. Just go home, don't tell anybody about this event, and trust me: everything'll be all right.

LYNNETTE. I ain't gonna let ya go alone. We gon die together. Don' forget da blood we shared.

DAVID JR. [*Supplicating with a raised voice.*] I'm not gonna die. Going with you is gonna worsen everything up. I got a safe plan for all this. I promise, we gonna be back together very soon.

LYNNETTE. No baby, I ain't gonna leave ya alone in a jungle full of monstrous beasts. We gotta die together.

DAVID JR. [*Begging.*] Lynette, please, do as I explained to you after my dream.

There is dead silence. Lynnette seems to buy David Jr.'s pleas.

DAVID JR. Please, baby, please!

LYNNETTE. [*Nodding, after a short silence.*] Okay, baby! I wish ya good luck, baby!

DAVID JR. [*To Kalol.*] You can let her go now. She's a woman of her word. [*To Lynnette.*] Do as I explained to you after my dream.

Kalol releases Lynnette. David Jr. is walked to the exit with Apolosa and Kapoza still holding him by his arms. Kalol follows behind.

As soon as they leave, Lynnette walks by the exit and watches how they leave. The sound of a car's ignition is heard, as well as a car revving sound.
Lynnette takes her phone and dials 911.

LYNNETTE. [To *herself.*] He told me not to call the police. But I gotta do it, anyway.
PHONE [*Answering message*]. You have reached the Aerosanam emergency line. We are experiencing a high volume of calls right now. Please leave a detailed message and your phone number, and one of our operators will return your call. Otherwise, you can call back later. Leave a message after the beep.

Lynnette hangs up her cell phone. After couple seconds, she redials.

LYNNETTE. [*While the phone is ringing, pleading softly.*] Please don't fail me.
PHONE [*Answering message.*] You have reached—

Lynnette hangs up and dials 911 again.

LYNNETTE. [*Getting an attitude.*] If they ain't gon answer dis time, I'm break this damn phone.
PHONE. You have reached an Aerosanam 911 operator. Do you need the police or the fire department?
LYNNETTE. [*Relieved.*] The police, please!
PHONE. Can I put you on hold for just a second, please? Don't hang up on me, okay? It'll be for just a second.
LYNNETTE. Okay. [*She is losing patience. Even her gestures are showing impatience.*]
PHONE. [*After a few seconds.*] Sorry, ma'am. What's your location, please?
LYNNETTE. Three Quimange Avenue South, room seven.
PHONE. May I know what's going on, please?

LYNNETTE. Three lunatic people just kidnapped ma fiancé.

PHONE. Do you know who those people are?

LYNNETTE. I never saw 'em before. I'm new in this town. But I guess I got an idea where dey taking him up.

PHONE. Okay. There's an officer patrolling the area around your location. I'll send him to you right away.

LYNNETTE. Please! Thank you!

Lynnette sits down on the bed, holding her head between her hands. A couple seconds later, a knock on the door is heard. Lynnette stands up and walks to the exit. Andricoco, the police officer, enters.

ANDRICOCO. So they kidnapped your fiancé, huh?

LYNNETTE. Yeah! Three lunatic people—

ANDRICOCO. You don't need to tell me the story. I know everything.

LYNNETTE. How did you know?

ANDRICOCO. I work for your rival in love, Miss Arleta.

LYNNETTE. [*Holding her head and stepping back.*] What?

ANDRICOCO. [*Explaining.*] Everybody in Aerosanam works for the almighty Arleta.

LYNNETTE. [*Holding her hands on her chest.*] Oh my God!

ANDRICOCO. [*Sincerely.*] I envy you! You're the rival of the most powerful woman on earth.

LYNNETTE. [*Raising her hands up in prayer.*] God, please help. God, no human is more powerful than you are. I'm square scared. I'm really scared. Please, God, don't make my bad situation get worse. Help me, God, please! Amen.

ANDRICOCO. [*Patting her.*] Don't worry! I'm related to your mother-in-law.

LYNNETTE. I know you, Uncle Andricoco! You came to arrest me once, remember?

ANDRICOCO. [*Ignoring her remarks.*] I've been working with your mother to get you out of this infernal vortex. First off, be calm. Nothing'll happen to David Jr. He's being taken to Arleta; then he'll be released afterward. [*From his pocket, he takes out an ID card and hands it to Lynette.*] This'll be your new identification card.

LYNNETTE. [*Observing the card.*] It's a man!

ANDRICOCO. Don't worry about the gender. Just memorize that name. It'll be yours until you leave Aerosanam.

LYNNETTE. Raymond Greathouse.

ANDRICOCO. That's right! Starting today, you are now Mr. Greathouse. Forget about Lynnette Zibo.

LYNNETTE. Ma name is Raymond Greathouse. Raymond Greathouse. Are you sure I ain't gonna forget it? How come ya din't pick somethin' easy, like a name of a celebrity, Marilyn Monroe, for example, or just any other easy name to remember?

ANDRICOCO. [*Ignoring her remarks.*] Now pack your belongings.

LYNNETTE. All I have is just that backpack. [*She points at a backpack on the floor.*] That's all my and David belongings.

ANDRICOCO. I'm gonna take you to a close friend of mine. A makeup artist. She already has the instructions. She'll metamorphose you into a man. Once released from Arleta, your fiancé'll join you there shortly. He'll be metamorphosed into a lady. [*Lynnette opens wide her eyes and mouth.*] Don't worry. It isn't gonna be neither a plastic surgery nor a sex reassignment surgery. Only your appearance'll change. You'll look like Raymond Greathouse on that ID, and your fiancé will look like this. [*He takes out another ID card and hands it to Lynnette.*]

LYNNETTE. [*Stunned.*] Oh my God! Miss Screna Palmer! [*She points her major finger at the photo ID and smile broadly.*] This is awesome!

ANDRICOCO. Wrong finger!

Lynnette changes her pointing finger and points at the photo ID with her index finger.

ANDRICOCO. Here in Aerosanam, we use the major finger as an insult. Especially when we wanna say the "F" word.

LYNNETTE. [*Smiling.*] Sorry, I ain't from here.
ANDRICOCO. Time to go, girl.
LYNNETTE. Boy!
ANDRICOCO. [*Clearing his throat.*] Sorry! Time to go, Mr. Greathouse.

They walk toward the exit.

Curtain.

SCENE 3
In Arleta's living room.

Curtain opens. Arleta is sitting in her special throne-chair. Five feet away from her, David Jr. is held on the floor by Apolosa and Kapoza, belly down, arms spread apart.

ARLETA. [*Commanding calmly.*] Bring him to me.

Kapoza and Apolosa help David Jr. to stand up. They bring him closer to Arleta. David Jr.'s face is full of bruises. Apolosa and Kapoza leave. Kalol enters and brings a box of napkins to Arleta and then leaves.

ARLETA. Bring your face closer, please. [*David Jr. leans forward. She cleans his face with a tissue.*] Oh my poor baby! I'm sorry that you got hurt... Love sometimes has to put you through hardships and many oops in order to accept it. [*She keeps wiping his face slowly.*] I'm not asking you to love me if you can't... You probably love to death your Lynnette Zibo... But don't force me to eliminate her without trial. [*David Jr. opens his eyes and looks steadily at her, startled.*] Don't worry! I'm capable of wiping her out. But I won't make her disappear, because of you, just for you, because you love her. [*David relaxes.*] My problem isn't because you love her... Both of you guys have been saying that you drunk each other's blood and promised that you'll stick together forever in your lives. [*She stands up and continues to wipe his face.*] My problem is to accomplish what God told me to do... I can't ignore it. The will of God is so powerful that I can't walk away from it. [*Pause.*] Lemme ask you one more time. Can you marry me, please? [*Silence.*]

David Jr. is looking straight at her, like a statue. He doesn't move.

ARLETA. [*She keeps wiping his face.*] Abraham agreed to sacrifice his unique son, Isaac, because God asked him to. I'll do everything possible to accomplish the will of God… Sarah, in the Bible, got pregnant when she was ninety-five. I can do the same at seventy… In this big city, I'm second to none. I grant wishes to every single citizen of Aerosanam. Why can't I grant anything to myself?

David Jr. is not saying a word. Arleta puts the box of tissues away. David Jr. stands straight.

ARLETA. [*Walking around David.*] Don't think, because I'm begging you to marry me, that I'm not able to force you to marry me. [*Sigh.*] Now, stay quiet the next time I speak to you, and I'll give orders to have your ugly girlfriend Lynnette wiped out.

DAVID JR. [*Speaking fast and begging.*] Not her, please. Don't mingle her between me and you. You've tortured my mind and emotions, I accept. I beg you to keep your torture to me only. This matter doesn't concern Lynnette. Just leave her alone. She's innocent.

ARLETA. [*With enthusiasm.*] You're obsessed with her; that's why you're rejecting me.

DAVID JR. [*Normally.*] If you want me to be your husband, then you gotta leave me the direction of this affair. Traditionally, it's a man who proposes to a woman.

ARLETA. This is beyond the scope of tradition. It's about accomplishing the will of God.

DAVID JR. [*He walk close to Arleta's char and hit his fist on the chair's arm, yelling.*] Stop telling me about God. You can't be fooling me and everybody that God spoke to you. You just a schizophrenic woman listening to her own thoughts.

ARLETA. [*Very calm.*] Calm down. There's no need to show off higher emotions for such little demand… If you don't believe that you're the chosen one, why did I leave millions of men around here and just fell on you? I never seen you before. I never heard a name of David Schumerman before I heard it from God. [*Slight pause.*] Now I'm your gift from God. Please, can you marry me?

DAVID JR. [*Indignantly.*] It's complicated! [*Pause.*] You making sound easy as if everybody should easily accept your thoughts.

ARLETA. Those aren't thoughts but facts.

DAVID JR. [*Sadly.*] If you're a fact-lover, then you should not be forcing me to marry you. It's against facts. It's against natural order. It doesn't smell love. [*Silence.*] I see! You're forcing me to marry you in order to re-generate your energy to work against the chaos of your own body?

ARLETA. I can't rely on your energy to rejuvenate. [*Deep breath.*] I'm not a pedophile. I know there are hundreds of young gerontophiles around Aerosanam. There're young males to help me restore what you think. I can have anybody that I need in a minute. But in my entire life, I swallowed it only three times. I'm like a virgin. So you'll never have any problem with me… Between me and you, it's all about love.

DAVID JR. You're on the wrong side of love. Like a farmer, you are turning my family into a spoiled crop.

ARLETA. Oh poor David. You only see the wrong side of the coin… Why? [*Slight pause.*] I'm suggesting you to flip it, please. Contemplate life to the fullest extent and find that every moment is just a celebration of life. It's a treasure… Life is really a true treasure.

DAVID JR. [*He shakes his head.*] It ain't gonna work with me.

David Jr. looks around the room. He realizes that there is nobody else except him and Arleta. He pulls off her glasses, then runs away toward the exit. Arleta looks at him as he tries to escape. She shakes her head, crosses her arms across her chest, and smiles.

As soon as David Jr. gets closer to the exit, his mother, Linzi Longfen, walks in. David Jr. stops. He is stunned. Linzi enters, shaking her head.

LINZI. [*Pointing at Arleta, a sign to David Jr. to return.*] I ain't gonna allow you to run away this time.

DAVID JR. [*Backing up and speaking with deep concern.*] Mom! Was it you? All this time, was it you, the one who has been selling me here? [*Shaking his head.*] I can't believe that this's happening.

LINZI. [*Commanding.*] Go back to meet your fiancée.

DAVID JR. [*Still shaking his head, stunned.*] It was you, Mother, playing all those games? You made me my sister an enemy 'cause I mistakenly thought it was her who was spying on me...

LINZI. [*With great confidence.*] What a woman can do better than any creature is to keep a secret.

DAVID JR. [*Still backing off to the slow pace of her mother's steps,* and still shaking his head.] I still don't believe my eyes. And I think everybody in this town is gonna faint... Mom, lemme ask you again, was it you, the spy working against her own son? Was it really you?

LINZI. [*Nodding, triumphant, and advancing forward.*] Yeah! It's been me. You were wrong when you accused your sister Kassandra of spying on you. I was the one. [*Slight pause. David Jr. is still walking backward slowly, and Linzi is advancing slowly as well.*] I've been working for Arketta since her mother picked you to be her future husband. I was refusing to allow you to marry her only 'cause your father was opposed. I never want the entire family to know that the parents were divided in this issue. It happened that when I and your father were in our bedroom alone, I begged him to allow this union between you and Arleta to happen. But he showed his toughness. He never wanted it to happen. However, when we were discussing this whole business in the family, I did my best to ally with your father's point of view in order to keep the family harmony.

DAVID JR. [*Still backing up, step by step.*] Are you really doing this to me, your lovely son?

LINZI. It's for your benefit, son. As your mother, the only thing I wish for you is a better and successful life. That's been my dearest dream ever since I conceived you... I can't let this opportunity of a lifetime get away from you.

DAVID JR. Why then did you bring Lynnette here to Aerosanam to join and marry me?

LINZI. That was just a diversion, a plan intended to keep you in the dark. I never wanted you to know the role I was playing on your behalf.

Up There to Step

DAVID JR. [*Bitterly.*] I hate you, Mom! I really heart you. [*Near tears.*] You know that you're the one behind all this bogeyman business. You know better that since day one, when I and Lynnette fell in love, you were so badly opposed. For two long years, you fought our love like daily war and you hounded Lynnette like a skunk… It was your decision to move to Aerosanam in order to run away from her… Once in Aerosanam, all this Arleta account opened. Just because of you… You are the one who started all this… Now, after you've put me in the mouth of a ferocious anaconda, you tapping your chest to be a true woman, able to keep secrets... I hate you, Mama. I Hate. The anaconda of Arleta is ready to swallow me, and she's threatening to kill Lynnette…

They come close to where Arleta is standing and stop. They form a little circle of three.

LINZI. [*Calmly.*] You have Mom's blessings to marry Arleta.
DAVID JR. I can't do it without Dad's approval. Convince Dad to accept the deal. I won't hesitate if both of my parents agree. Parents are a child's God here on earth.
LINZI. I can say some secret about you that'll dry your mouth for so long.
DAVID JR. Say it.
LINZI. Your father's signed his approval already.
DAVID JR. Bring it.

Linzi looks at Arleta, who nods. She claps two times. Kalol enters with a sheet of paper. She hands it to Arleta and then leaves. Arleta hands the paper to Linzi, who hands it to David Jr.

DAVID JR. [*After reading the paper.*] I need the signature of my father. Not of his friend.
LINZI. It's your father's signature.
DAVID JR. The only signature I see here is that of Iberkonta Denis, my father's best friend. [*He turns the paper around to see if there are notes. Then he shakes the paper.*] Where's my father's signature?

97

LINZI. It's time to face the truth, David. What a woman is able to do better than any creature is to preserve a secret. You're grown already, and you're about to marry; you gotta learn the truth. [*Slight pause.*] Starting today, know that David Schumerman Sr. is not your father!

DAVID JR. [*Choking.*] What?

LINZI. Lemme introduce to you your biological father. [*Pause.*] Iberkonta Denis.

Linzi dramatically gestures toward the stage right entrance. Iberkonta Denis enters, smiling. David Jr. falls down, simulating fainting. Iberkonta comes to where David Jr. fell and helps him to stand up.

IBERKONTA. [*Helping David Jr. to stand up.*] Stand up, David! Stand up.

DAVID JR. [*Holding his head after standing up.*] Is this really happening? It's a dream, right? [*He looks at Linzi and then at Iberkonta.*] When I wake up, all this'll be gone, right? The reality will continue as before, right?

IBERKONTA. This isn't a dream. I'm your true biological father. And you have my blessing to proceed with your marriage.

Kalol enters with another sheet of paper and hands it to David Jr.

KALOL. Just in case you don't believe, here's the DNA test. Your mother did it when you were a boy. [*She exits.*]

DAVID JR. [*Examining the paperwork, perplexed.*] Mom, what did you do? You cheated on my father?

LINZI. Thank God that that's not your problem.

IBERKONTA. It's a long story, son. You'll get details and developments as the days progress.

DAVID JR. Mom! Say something, please. You're getting my head big.

LINZI. That's one of the women-exclusive specialties. They act for the best interest of their boys. You never grew up with regard for your mother.

There is a pause. Everybody stays quiet for couple seconds. Then Arketta enters and approaches the little group.

ARKETTA. [*Standing akimbo, with a bossy attitude and tone. She gives orders.*] Now that we have a deal, my mother's wedding'll take place forty-eight hours from now. [*Iberkonta and Linzi nod.*] We gotta set everything up and have invitations sent...Is there any questions? [*Silence.*] You're all dismissed.

Curtain.

SCENE 4
Betsy enters.

BETSY [*Frowning and speaking with a tone of dissatisfaction.*]. I hate speaking in public. I'm shy and I believe I'll have a panic attack. Or I'll end up freezing like a mammoth. [*She pauses and shakes her head.*] I don't even know if I can do this. [*She rubs her belly.*] But, for the sake of the lovely child inside my belly, I'll do the impossible. [*Pause.*] I've been asked to speak at Arleta's wedding ceremony about dreams, in exchange for a check of several thousand dollars. [*She raises her head and hands up in a prayer posture.*] Thanks God and allow everything to work for me for the sake of my baby. [*She rubs her belly again.*] I'll probably not be a beggar anymore after this speech. But, I'm scared. [*She puts a hand on her chest.*] Oh My God, my heart is beating fast like that of a fetus. [*She takes couple deep breaths.*] Okay, let's do this. [*She adjusts herself.*] This speech was written by father Antonio Moretti, who has become a very good friend of mine since the time I went to beg for food at his place. [*Smile.*] Thanks God that I have a gift of memorization... I have memorized the entire speech, word after word. [*Deep breaths.*] I hope it's gonna work for me in public. [*She clears her throats twice.*] Here we go! [*She adjusts her posture and stays straight and concentrated.*] Ladies and gentlemen, welcome to this wedding ceremony. Let's talk about dreams. [*Pauses. She speaks now with confidence.*]

It is said that at the beginning was the word, the word was with God and that everything that was made, was made with the word. However, little or nothing is said about what was before the beginning. [*She looks around.*] Has anybody ever asked himself about what existed before the beginning? [*Silence.*] Dreams! Before the beginning were dreams. The word come later. Dreams are what make each one of us similar to God. [*Sigh.*] God is a dreamer because most of the creation didn't start spontaneously. It was first dreamed ...

One law has been omitted in every book of law. It's the law of dreams or law of chance. From it, the creative process start. Today, Arleta could not have this marriage if she didn't dream it

We live in a big dream. This world is all about dreams. Can you imagine a life without dreams? [*Sighs.*] Awful! It would be awful, dark, and scary. [*Breath.*] If there were no dreams, no inventions could ever had taken place. No evolution, no progress, and no discovery could ever had happened. All could had been just *status quo*. No fire, no electricity, no computer or not even this play could ever had materialized.

There is music and dance of dreams. Sing and dance it ahead of anything. Put it in front of your family, in front of your life and in front of your health. In doing so, you'll see how easily you handle your family, your life and your health. Because you just put yourself in the position of a creator, and you just kept your creativity alive. [*Breath.*] In your dreams, you are your own doctor. You can heal yourself as well as accomplish miracles. [*Breath.*] Dreams are golden standard currency of life.

Some people do many things it take to create and accomplish a dream. Whether a dream come up as images during sleep or as an intuition, an inspiration, a plan, a goal, or as a voice, like in the case of Arleta who heard a voice of God urging her to marry David Schumerman, it is first the precursor of everything. A dream is a creative act by the dreamer because most dreams come from inside out. Some external events or words may also inspire a dreamer to start creating his own dreams.

Dreams are up there to step. You can step anywhere in the dream world--your dream worlds, with the opportunity to grab not only just one creative word, but also multiple jobs. There is much to dream than anything else. There is an unlimited sea of dreams. There is always one more dream to live. So, I urge you to dive into the sea of your dreams and don't take the swimming lightly.

No dream happen to you but dreams happen for you. If you stop dreaming you stay behind. You can't live in the present when you only dream from the past. You stay behind, looking in the future from a past perspective. You stay in Antiquity.

When two dreams compete, or better, when two dreamers compete, there is no protagonist, and no antagonist. There is no hero, and no villain. There is no reason not to try the unthinkable. The strongest dreamer may take it all. For those who dream big, there will be more dreams added to their worlds. Those who dream recklessly will be wrested even the modicum of their dreams…

She stops briskly and rubs her belly.

BETSY. [*Plaintively.*] My belly! [*She holds her belly, calling out for help, worried and creaming.*] Somebody help, please. [*Sitting slowly on the floor.*] I think the baby is coming out before my due date. [*Screaming.*] Somebody help, please… I'm delivering… Somebody help, please…

Curtain.

SCENE 5

A celebration room, decorated for a wedding ceremony.

Curtain opens. There are people sitting in the chairs. A wedding song is play-ing. People are dressed up. David Jr.'s parents are present. Kassandra and Jevus sit around another table. Belgina is seated alone. Her husband is the MC. Arketta is sitting with Kapoza and Apolosa.

After about five seconds, Kish enters with a microphone.

KISH. Ladies an' gentlemen, good evening, an' welcome to dis tremen-dous an' unforgettable wedding ceremony. My name is Kish Kyaleza. I work at Beautify Aerosanam, a private company owned an' managed by yo humble servitor tonight, [*sigh*] myself. It's my distinguished honor to be your MC this evening...Da city of Aerosanam is vested in its highest outfits, an' it's goldenly decorated in its highest color as it celebrates da rite of matrimonial union of one who's considered by all to be da mother of this town. [*There is a standing ovation. Kish stops and waits for the ovation to settle.*] Arleta Yavanov has spent billions out of her pocket for da develop-ment an' growth of Aerosanam. [*Another ovation.*] Her generous donations to dis city speak loud through its works. Aerosanam's filled with schools, hospitals, an' many livin' complexes, to name just a few dat a' the fruits of Miss Arleta. [*Ovation.*] Today, Aerosanam'll witness da change on the title it uses for Arleta. After dis grandiose ceremony, our Arleta no longer be refereed as miss. She be Mrs. Schumerman. [*Standing ovation.*] Ladies an' gentlemen, 'low me to introduce to y'all da man who be officiatin' dis ceremony, [*He raises his voice and pauses after word*] Father Antonio Moretti.

There is a standing ovation. The priest enters, waves to the people.

KISH. Now, ladies an' gentlemen, help me in welcomin' yo bride, the mother of Aerosanam, accompanied by Miss Kalol-- [*Raising his voice.*] Arleta Yavanov.

There is a long-standing ovation, with whistling and Arleta's name being called out loud. Arleta enters, wearing a white wedding dress. Kalol is behind her. Arleta waves to the attendees and receives a wave back. A voice is heard from the guests: "We love you, Arleta." She stands a couple feet to the front and left of the priest.

KISH. Thanks, guys, for showing yo love to Arleta, da mother of Aerosanam. Now show yo love in welcomin' the man who be soon called the father of Aerosanam, accompanied by his best man Iberkonta Denis, the groom—[*He raises his voice.*] David Schumerman Jr.

There is a standing ovation that is cut short by the lone apparition of Iberkonta Denis. He enters, showing signs and gestures of concern. Iberkonta walks to Kish. He whispers something in one of his ears. Kish asks him to repeat it. Iberkonta whispers again. Kish frowns hard, then nods. Iberkonta whispers to Arleta and the priest, then goes to stand a couple in front and right side of the priest.
There is a commotion in the little group.

KISH. [*Coldly.*] Ladies an' gentlemen, please remain seated. We be playin' some wedding songs before we continue with our matrimonial ceremony.

A wedding song starts playing. Arketta stands up and walks up front to talk to Iberkonta. She is followed by Kapoza and Apolosa. After talking to Iberkonta, she talks to her mother. She gives orders to Kapoza, who nods, and then exits. Arketta gives orders to both Antonio and Kish. They nod. Kish talks to the priest, then speaks on the microphone while the wedding song is still playing. Arketta leaves her table, walks to where Kish is standing. Kapoza exits.

KISH. Ladies and gentlemen, it's time for me to return da favor to you for 'lowing me to be your MC today. As I said before, dis the biggest honor of my life to be your MC today—

Arketta takes the microphone from Kish and addresses the group.

ARKETTA. [*Authoritatively.*] Cut the music, please. [*She waits a couple seconds.*] Ladies and gentlemen, please remain seated. I'm in charge of this wedding ceremony. And starting now, I'll be your MC... There's a little bad news, but trust me, I won't disappoint you all. [*There is a commotion. The attendees are in shock.*] The groom is missing from his dressing room. [*The commotion grows louder. People talk to each other and express their emotions. She stays quiet for a short while. Then she continues.*] Again, gimme a couple of minutes as my services are trying to locate the groom and our ceremony will continue shortly. [*She looks around.*] DJ, please play the music while I fix the situation.

A wedding song plays. Kish walks toward the tables and finds a seat next to his wife, Belgina. The priest, the bride, Kalol, and Iberkonta are standing at the same place, waiting patiently.

Kapoza reenters. He whispers something in Arketta's ear. Arketta nods and, using gestures and whispers, gives some orders. Kapoza gives her a folder, which she keeps. Then Kapoza leaves.

ARKETTA. Dear invitees! Just an update on our missing groom. He's nowhere to be found in this building... He isn't in the vicinity either... Hang on, please. He shortly gonna be found around Aerosanam... I have people working for me in every corner of this town. [*Slight pause.*] You guys came here for a wedding ceremony. I apologize for the low standard that it's showing so far. Again, I ask for your indulgence. I'm gonna shift the gears up very soon.

Linzi Longfen, who was sitting quietly as if nothing were happening, stands up.

LINZI. [*To Arketta.*] You don't need to search for my son in Aerosanam. It'll be a big waste of time. Please tell your guests to go back home. The wedding ceremony should, at this time, be shamefully ended.
ARKETTA. What makes you believe that your son won't be found?

LINZI. [*Triumphant.*] What a woman can do better than anybody else is to play a diversion game well and efficiently. [*Sighs.*] I made you believe that I was working for you. [*She shakes her head.*] The truth is that I was just diverting your stinky mind. I made myself able to learn the ways you run your business around in order to destroy you from your root, and to make you ashamed in front of all the people of this city who adore you like an angel. [*Sigh.*] Since the very beginning, I was opposed to your so-called God recommendation for your mother to marry my young boy. If it isn't witchcraft, what else you think it is? Satanism? Demonology? [*She holds her hands out, palms facing up, shaking them.*] You probably know better than I do. A seventy-year-old lady, to coerce into marriage a seventeen-year-old boy? Come on, lady! Stop lying in God's name, please! God's word is naturally the holiest you can think about. It can't direct you to act wrong or against the morality and the standard of society. [*Sigh.*] It's just a shame for a woman like you, believed to be the most powerful woman on the planet, to lie in the name of God. The other odd thing is, if it really came from God, you couldn't've spent millions, coercing and buying the faith of many, in order to force the little poor boy to marry your mother. [*Sigh.*] The light you needed your mother to suck from him, either in order to stay alive longer or in order to increase your wealth and power, is gone now. [*Sigh.*] I've put you against the wall… Now prove me wrong and show everybody that it's God who has given you what you wanted. [*Slight pause.*] My son flew off twenty minutes ago, using a female fake identity and girl makeup. My son is now off the radar. He may only be found in the twilight zone. [*She chuckles.*] To be precise, he'll be soon enjoying his nuptial night in New Oceania, where he's now flying with his fiancée, Lynnette Zibo.

The scene remains quiet for a short while.. Linzi breaks the silence.

LINZI. I've put you against the wall. [*She looks triumphantly around the crowd.*] I'm suggesting you go peer at yourself in a mirror—a mirror of shame. You might get a chance to see how reddened and wide open your eyes are right now. Tell me out loud, please. [*She laughs.*] Your eyes have reddened more than that of a ferret. Your eyes are more rounded than those of an owl. They're popping out more than those of a viper. You look as if you are wearing special contacts designed by the devil's ophthalmologist. [*Chuckles.*] Now that I've been able to put shame in your soul, you look like the offspring of a relationship between a ferret, an owl, and a viper. Red, rounded, and popping-out eyes—what a perfect combination! [*Pause*] What a shame! The Iron Lady of Aerosanam is being humiliated in her own so-called kingdom. [*Chuckles.*] See how shamefully you're sweating, like a running lion that misses catching its prey. And soon you'll be screaming like a woman in labor. [*Sigh.*] All your makeup is melting like ice in sublimation. Your lips are dry like the sands of a desert that has not received droplets for millenniums. [*Sigh.*] I suggest that you rub your lips on the floor to wet them up a little bit. The floor is moister. It might help your lips regain their original appearance. [*Laughs.*] I ain't gonna leave here until I witness how your brain's gonna fart to save this unknown dark ceremony that you've been shamefully calling a wedding for your spoiled sandwich mother. [*Chuckles.*] You look like a widow who lost her husband before even marrying him. What an enigma! [*She looks around to assess the group. There is a deathly silence.*] I understand why they call you mommy-sitter. You've been passing dirty clothes and spoiled food to the Aerosanam people. You've brainwashed them to believe in your so-called generosities. [*Head shake.*] Not anymore! [*Pause.*] Aerosanam ain't a concentration camp where everybody has to wear an Arketta-fashioned spacesuit in order to breathe the colored carbon dioxide coming out of her bruised lungs. [*She shakes her head and finger.*] Nobody's supposed to bend his body every time Arketta nods her head. [*Pointing at Arketta.*] I've proven to every soul that you aren't an Aerosanam babysitter. [*She stops. Since the room remains silent, she continues.*]

You said stars from the sky told your mom to marry my son, right? Do you really believe that the stars are really blind for attempting to link an old bastard of seventy years to a seventeen-year-old angel? [*Slight pause.*] For years, you sat relaxed on Aerosanam's genitals... You've bullied so many innocent souls with your wealth. Until you tried to trip over a platinum woman, and she's now putting you on the edge of your own ruin. [*She hits her chest with a fist.*] I'm the destroyer of queens, and I'm the house of fire. Ask those who grew up along with me. They'll narrate my stories that'll leave your mouth wide open for a long period never recorded in the history of humankind. My exploits will steal your sleep indefinitely and fill your heart with jealousy. [*A couple deep breaths.*] Your so-called God made a mistake in choosing my family as your bait. He's failed... This whole event should teach you how to avoid to use your own God against somebody else's God, life, and family... Your plan to marry a seventeen-year-old is not only impossible but also absurd and ridiculous. In doing so, you made me able to change the landscape of Aerosanam. Everybody who believed in your unlimited and invincible powers will be demystified starting today. [*Pause.*] I ain't gonna leave here. I ain't gonna retreat. I'll stick around till I see how you gonna put an end to this spoiled ceremony. I'll see how you gonna buy victory in this particular circumstance: Is it gonna be a miracle from your so-called God or from your money? [*Slight pause.*] The name Arleta doesn't bear any special vibration, yet every member of the Aerosanam community fears it. I'm Moses, the savior, and I'll remind you of the story of Peter, who denied Jesus. The rooster did sing "cocorico" three times to remind him of his blunder. Same way today, I'm singing "cocorico" like a rooster to remind you of all your sins you've committed against this city. You've denied your humanity in favor of your wealth. You'll remember this day for the rest of your life. Even after you die, you'll remember this day for eternity. [*Pause.*]

Because the noose you had over Aerosanam's neck is cut. I'm tossing your damn soul away, into the eternal fire where it belongs. I'm like the sun raising the mercury in the thermometer of Aerosanam and wiping the veil of slavery off this city. Long live freedom in Aerosanam. [*She gestures to ask support of the attendees.*] Everybody, please repeat after me: Long live freedom in Aerosanam. [*Silence.*] Long live freedom in Aerosanam. [*Nobody backs her. There is dead silence.*] Come on, guys. Don't be scared. She isn't a god. [*Silence. She stays quiet. All her courage is gone.*]

BELGINA. [*To Kish in a lower tone and voice.*] I think she hasn't tasted yet the "yes, ma'am" recipe that everybody in Aerosanam enjoys, right? That's the only dish cooked with endless love by the worshiped Arketta. Has she?

KISH. [*He shakes his head and whispers.*] Not yet! She's underestimated her. I'm afraid that she be tasting Arketta's recipe hard way. Nobody toys with the Great Arketta.

LINZI. [*She's shocked but speaks courageously to the attendees.*] You are afraid of her? Arketta isn't a god. We need a revolution. I'm the small match able to kindle a big fire. Let's do this, guys. [*Nobody reacts. She speaks to Arketta.*] The words are still warm in your wet mouth. The crimes you committed might be forgiven. Open your stinky mouth to confess your sins; then go to the Aerosanam River to bathe seven times for your purification and rejuvenation. This is a time for redemption before all these people turn against you to stone you up. [*The silence continues.*] For two generations, Aerosanam residents've been mercilessly tossed in the air and have been falling on ground that's filled with Arleta and Arketta's stinky shit. I appreciate a lot Belgina, who didn't follow the footsteps of both her mother and grandmother. I hope with her, after those two evils are gone, will come the end of the tyranny that has blinded Aerosanam's people. I can't wait to see that happening. [*She clears her throat.*] Curiously, almost every Aerosanam resident has bruises, broken legs, broken hips, and broken backbones as the result of being constantly tossed into the air by Arketta. But they still worship her after she fixes what she has damaged. They keep saying that she's the mother of Aerosanam because of all the charities of her making. They call her smart. [*She laughs.*] I really can't wait to get out of here.

Arketta, who was quietly listening to Linzi, adjusts herself and clears her throat.

BELGINA. [*She gestures at Arketta not to respond.*] Mom, I got this. Since she mentioned my name, lemme teach her an emperor's lesson. [*To Linzi, pointing at her.*] Life has only one face-- And that's yourself. You may believe that my mom abuses her people. However, look around and see how they laughing at you... Aerosanam people will put you on the table, ready to wash away the glorious veil of illusion that blinds your view. [*She clears her throat.*] Actually, life has two faces: you and your own image. The latter may have an appearance of my mother, or anybody else. [*Breath.*] You're armed with great intentions like Don Quixote, but the veil of illusion has played a big game to the point that you fighting against windmills and wrongly measuring the superpowerful Arketta against your low standard. [*Breath.*] There's nobody to blame but yourself. [*Breath.*] I'll give you some techniques to use when you are playing a game: remember to apply the defensive... I mean don't just attack... Know to defend yourself too. It works in every game. [*Breath.*] Know to survive. [*Breath.*] There's no defeat or failure. What looks like failure is just a stumbling block for a better outcome for the future. Failure and victory are all made from the same broadcloth; they are helping to drive the lessons your way. [*Breath.*] Needless to say that it's not my mother that tosses Aerosanam people into air but their own survival instinct that does. They accept responsibility to be tossed into the air, and they do not blame anybody but themselves. [*Breath.*] Cut your hair bald, Linzi. You'll be ugly like the emperor moth. However, that will help the butterfly in you to rise from the cocoon, and you'll be born again, the new Linzi. [*Breath.*] The fear of losing your son made you take measures that are disastrous for yourself. I can't teach your mind. Your glorious veil of illusion is shining so darkly that it blinds you to the thousands of folds. [*Linzi starts to say something, but Belgina stops her with a hand gesture.*] The blind side is the survival instinct of the Aerosanam people to be tossed into the air because they are learning how to miss the ground. It's the only way they easily are facing up with themselves. So failure or broken bones are just steps toward their perfection. My mom has nothing to do with none of your accusations.

LINZI. She is. People like you and her need to star in a TV show and have characters Dr. House diagnose their delusional thoughts.

BELGINA. I understand that you just moved to Aerosanam. You stayed quite close to my mom, and you worked for her. You didn't really learn that she ain't an ordinary woman, did you? What a demonic curse on yourself!

LINZI. I know that your mom is a fallen angel. I learned that truth when I worked for her. My sole purpose, though, was to learn the ways of a viper that she is, in order to whop her head with my heel. It's the fulfillment of the prophecy. A woman will crush snakes like you, a fallen angel.

BELGINA. [*Calmly.*] You're rolling problems on your toes. Your feet will get heavier. You may find yourself unable to run afterward.

LINZI. So are you!

BELGINA. [*Very calm.*] You taking courage to hurt yourself by defying a fallen angel. Why?

LINZI. Because you've been hammering me over my loved ones.

BELGINA. You took voluntarily my mom's money.

LINZI. You bite me once, you can't bite me twice. [*Chuckles.*] I stayed closer to your mother in order to diagnose her bullying habits. I've found that she has cancer of vanity that's rapidly metastasizing. I had to prescribe a strong dose of chemotherapy to save her from infecting every other cell of her body. I had to save Aerosanam in the process.

BELGINA. Say it again?

LINZI. [*She looks at Arketta.*] I've diagnosed your foolish ailment as cancer of vanity. I'm gonna prescribe a strong dose of chemotherapy to cure you.

BELGINA. Good job, Doctor! Lemme just remind you that money always stands tall. Upgrade your disturbing mind, lady. Just learn not to accept money and try to run away... If you try to escape, money will have the right to stand very tall on you. My mom's rich and highly capable of things you can't even dream of in your entire life.

LINZI. [*To Arketta.*] I suggest you not rationalize that "I'm rich" and "I'm billionaire." You're hiding behind something that ain't you. Those're external belongings and diminish your humanity. I need to confront you as a human being. The true woman that I am versus the fake woman that you are. I can tell, by the way you looking at me, that besides your wealth, there's nothing left of you. Your identification with money—that's all is left of you. It's a shame. People like you should be weeded out by natural selection. You don't fit within ordinary mortals.

BELGINA. [*Calmly.*] You keep singing the same karaoke that Judas sang when he sold his master, Jesus of Nazareth. Who'll you finally blame when you decide to hang yourself as Judas did? Yourself, right?

LINZI. [*To Arketta.*] You're so arrogant, Iron Lady of Aerosanam. I'll tell you one thing: the only thing that matches your arrogance and your so-called power is your ignorance. [*She raises both index fingers and puts them on either side of her head, pointing up, to simulate horns.*] You're evil. You're evil. [*She turns about, showing the horns to the attendees.*] You're evil. [*She stops.*]

BELGINA. Is that all? I want more, please. Can you do it again, please? [*All the attendees say, "Do it again, do it again," waving their fists.*]

LINZI. [*Addressing the attendees, she points at Arketta.*] You see how I've clamped her mouth shut? [*To Arketta.*] Aerosanam ain't your kindergarten foundation. You can't control everybody, especially me. [*To the attendees.*] I'm an agent of Jesus, and he stands for y'all oppressed people in Aerosanam. He's your brother. So let's see how she's gonna save the day. There're hundreds of thousands of people in this world watching this event live on TV. [*To Arketta.*] Now, please show me, powerful Arketta, with what tissue do you wipe your behind?

Silence.

LINZI. That gives you a good feeling, right? I'm loving every second of it. I'm proud to have brought shame to you. [*Pause.*] I'm calling you and your mother out. You are both sellouts. [*Pause.*] You gotta dig more into your so-called extra power to save your mother's hypothetically biggest day. Otherwise, I'll send you deeply packing. It's a debacle in the making.

She stops and looks around. A short silence reigns. Arketta breaks it.

ARKETTA. Are you through with your heartened discourse, or you've got more to say?

[*Very calm.*] Did you finish?

LINZI. You want more? I do have more in my store, and—

ARKETTA. [*Very calm.*] Enough, lady, enough! Congratulations on your landslide short-lived victory. Now it's time for you to learn and enjoy the disturbing taste and price of deception.

David Sr., who was staying quiet, stands and whispers in Linzi's ear.

DAVID SR. Excuse me, baby. I'm going to the men's room.

Linzi nods. David Sr. leaves his seat and exits.

ARKETTA. [*To the guests.*] Sorry, guys, for the inconvenience. It's time to move on now. [*She clears her throat.*] *A malin, malin et demi*, say the French people. What a woman can do better than anybody else is to plan for a worst-case scenario... I'm doing this to show respect to my mother. Today's the greatest day of her life. She's been waiting for this moment for fifty-five years, after her first wedding when she was fifteen. [*To Linzi.*] Linzi, you can't just ruin it like that. I spent millions of dollars for this wedding and for your son to marry my mother. I bribed you millions to make this day happen. But you wanna raise your hand up and claim victory to the detriment of my mother? Unfortunately, you thought you were smart. But to a smart woman, I add another half. That makes me smart and one-half. So I planned carefully a plan B just in case there was a nightmare-case scenario. Don't blame me, because you did this to yourself. [*To the guests.*] Before I continue, lemme introduce to you the traitors.

Apolosa enters with Andricoco, Kapoza enters with Peta. Both are handcuffed. They are brought in front of Arketta. They are made to kneel. Andricoco is not in uniform. Linzi is shocked and can't believe her eyes.

ARKETTA. Dear distinguished guests, lemme present you two people who've attempted to spoil this ceremony. Andricoco helped the groom to escape by providing him a fake ID card and transportation to the airport. Peta Lubang is a makeup artist. She painted the face of our groom to look like a girl…For both our traitors, I've spent a lot of money on their education and the easiness of their lives… See how they're paying me back? See how they've betrayed the people of Aerosanam?

There is a commotion in the room. Arleta is very shocked, desperate. Arketta gives a sign to Kapoza and Apolosa, who walk the "prisoners" away. They exit.

ARKETTA. Before we proceed with our wedding ceremony, [*Arleta, who was desperate, opens her eyes wide and looks steadily at Arketta*], lemme briefly explain to everybody that my mother spent forty years asking God to send her the name of her husband, 'cause she was afraid to marry a husband who might not be hers. Therefore, recently, she heard the voice of God telling her that her husband's name is David Schumerman. We didn't know anybody with that name in Aerosanam. [*She slightly stops when Apolosa and Kapoza reenter and go occupy their seats.*] When we pushed on with our search, the mayor told us that there was a David Schumerman family that moved in Aerosanam just recently. So there were two Davids. We excluded David Sr. We negotiated with David Jr. and came to a deal for this wedding. However, God didn't tell us if the age of David mattered. He didn't say either if David will be senior or junior. So both were eligible to marry my mother. Then I found that Linzi wasn't officially married to David Sr. It was just a common-law marriage. [*To Linzi.*] Eh, Linzi, do you remember last time I made you sign some paperwork? Fortunately for me, you didn't read it. In one of those papers, you signed a waiver to your common-law marriage. [*She shows the paper to the attendees and waves it.*] It's notarized, and it says that [*she reads*] "I, Linzi Longfen, voluntarily agree to let David Schumerman marry Arleta Yavanov." It adds, "I never was married to David Schumerman, and I waive my common-law engagement to him." [*To the attendees.*] Ladies and gentlemen, the groom of Arleta Yavanov, David Schumerman Sr.

Up There to Step

An ovation is heard. The invitees stand and clap their hands as David Sr. enters and stands in front of Iberkonta, who has remained standing all this time. Linzi is very upset. She stands and tries to attack Arketta and everybody else. But Kish blocks her, and puts handcuffs on her.

LINZI. [*Yelling at Arketta.*] I know your profile. I know your weakness. I'll kill you. I'll kill you, Arketta. I'll motherfuck you up, I promise. I'll kill you, you sonofabitch. You're hijacking my man to profit your bitch mother? There're millions of single men around that match your mother's age. Can't you find them? Why did you destroy my family? Is it because you rich? Money, right? I'm suggesting you double your face because I'm gonna square it up. I'll kill you.

ARKETTA. You'll be covering corns, babe!

LINZI. What?

ARKETTA. I didn't mean to step on your toes, but you sneakily forced them under my foot. My feet are toe-killers. So am I. Miracle is what Arketta is made of.

LINZI. [*Yelling.*] You devil! You're worse than a combo of ten devils. You're destroying my family. What have I done to you? You're possessed by a terabyte demon. You're a hybrid between human and nonhuman.

ARKETTA. You wanted to oppose God's will.

LINZI. [*Still yelling.*] Don't lie in the name of God. The true God won't cause my lovely family to split. You heard the voice of the devil. You're the reincarnation of the devil. What made you choose only me among billions of people?

ARKETTA. You did this to yourself. You should've fought the war using your own means. But you accepted millions from my pocket; then you wanted to walk away triumphant, insulting and laughing at me.

LINZI. I didn't do it to myself. I was fighting to save my lovely son from the fisher's net that you forced him to be trapped in. You could've done the same if your son was trapped between the devil and the deep blue sea.

ARKETTA. Congratulations! You fought a good war. But your opponent was a millions times superior to you. You were like a baby born today challenging a wrestling champion in a fistfight. In doing so, you purchased your ticket to lose your husband. You put him in a danger zone. [*Breath.*] I do have the ability to suck blood like a vampire for the sake of justice. Lemme remind you that if you strike, I'll counterstrike. If a nail refuses to get in the wood, I strike more hammer blows.

LINZI. I'll kill you. I promise. I'll fuckin' kill you. [*To Arleta.*] If you think you're a powerful being, why did you rely on God to find you a husband? Why didn't you solve your celibacy problem by yourself? [*Slight pause.*] I'll kill you! I'll forcefully pull the shit out of your ass. I'll kill you! [*Pause.*] If I don't kill you, life will teach you better. Everything that you've done to me will come back to you and haunt your small ass. Life'll make you pay it with penalties, surcharges, and taxes above.

ARKETTA. You did this to yourself. Nobody else is to blame.

LINZI. This world is degrading because of people like you. Women used to trust their husbands but not anymore. They don't even allow them to talk on the phone because of people like you, thieves. [*Pause.*] God gave you Ten Commandments, in which the tenth says that you shall not covet. How the same God gonna tell you to steal my husband?

ARKETTA. [*Mockingly.*] I'll suggest you put on your first tattoo if you don't have one yet. On that tattoo, have the image of your so-called husband at a site you can look at and contemplate on him when you feel alone.

LINZI. You not worth living. You are like Judas of the Bible. Do you know your outcome? Judas ended by hanging himself because this world didn't belong to people like him as well as people like you.

ARKETTA. What may take you a lifetime in the making, I am able to realize in a second. Don't go around chasing after me. The faster and harder you chase me, the more I get away, and the more you hurt yourself.

LINZI. What could've happened to turn the hero of Aerosanam into a lunatic lady, stealing people's husbands?

ARKETTA. I spent millions for this moment, and that's how you were trying to walk away with both the money and the resolution to destroy my mother's biggest moment of her life?

LINZI. You are torturing me with the same degree of excitement that a devil uses. Do you ever assess your action? Or you're used only to run blindly like that on people?

ARKETTA. Those who oppose me end up turning themselves into my footsteps. In your case, you forgot to recharge the batteries. I possess a red button that can make shade without light.

LINZI. [*Lowering her voice.*] Oh my God! Tell me that this's not happening. Tell me that I'll wake up in the morning and take deep sigh of relief after knowing that it was just a dream. [*She screams.*] No, Arketta, you can't take my husband. You can't. [*She sobs.*]

ARKETTA. Keep dreaming! [*To Antonio.*] Father Antonio, you are in charge now.

Linzi is taken off of the stage. Arketta goes back to her seat. Antonio invites the couple to join him. David Sr. and Arleta come to stand in front of him.

ANTONIO. [*To the attendees.*] We are gathered here to celebrate a matrimonial union between David Schumerman Jr. and Arleta Yavanov. We ask God to help dem and bless deir union. [*To Arleta.*] Arleta Yavanov, do you accept David Schumerman as your lovely husband, to live togeder in a holy matrimonial marriage? Do you agree to love him, to obey him, honor him, be faithful to him, and keep him forever, for de worse and de good, as long as you will live togeder?

ARLETA. [*Smiling.*] Yes, I do. [*There is an ovation from the invitees.*]

ANTONIO. [*To David Sr.*] David Schumerman, do you accept Arleta Yavanov as your lovely wife, to live togeder in a holy matrimonial marriage? Do you agree to love her, to obey her, honor her, be faithful to her, and keep her forever, for de worse and de good, as long as you will live togeder?

DAVID SR. [*Smiling.*] Yes, I do.

There is a standing ovation from the invitees. The priest puts rings on David Sr. and Arleta. David Sr. opens Arleta's wedding veil. They kiss. After the ovation, Arketta takes the microphone.

ARKETTA. May I have your attention, please?

A couple seconds after, the calm is restored, and everybody pays attention to Arketta.

ARKETTA. [*Contented.*] Can we first give a big round of applause for my lovely mother, Arleta, please? [*The attendees applaud.*] Things are getting incredibly big here. As always, I tirelessly thrive to come up with some-thing new—something that never existed before. In my creative efforts, I came up with a special and outstanding event for my mother. I am good at defying the odds and changing deception into creativity; that's how I live. Since the creation of world, we've never seen what's gonna happen this evening. [*Sigh.*] I know all of you are curious and wanna hear as quickly as you can what I'm holding in my basket. Hang on, guys, we're almost there. [*Slight pause of suspense.*] Today, we gonna witness the wedding of a woman, my lovely mother, getting married to two men. This is a premier!

The group is shocked, and there is a huge silence. Some people open their eyes. Other open their mouths. Some have their hands over their open mouths, and others have their hands holding their heads or chests.

ARKETTA. Ladies and gentlemen, the second groom for my mother... [*She stays quiet for about five seconds.*]

There is suspense; the attendees hold their breath.

ARKETTA. Ladies and gentlemen, please welcome the second groom of Arleta, Misteeeer... [*Another five seconds of silence and suspense.*] I'm just kidding!

Everybody sighs, laughs, and talks about the joke.
  Kapoza exits. Seconds later he reenters. He whispers something to Arketta.

ARKETTA [*After a short while, she speaks using the microphone.*] May I have your attention, please? [*The stage get quiet.*] We have special speaker for this wedding ceremony. Please, helping me in welcoming... [*She pauses.*] Linzi Longfen.

Linzi enters, smiling, accompanied by Kish. She stands next to Arketta who hands the microphone to her.

LINZI [*Smiling*]. Hi everybody and sorry for my earlier attitude. [*She looks at Kish.*] Thank you for convincing me to speak at this ceremony. [*She waves a check.*] Thank you Kish for the big check of several million dollars. [*She looks at Arketta.*] Thank you Arketta. From you I've learned that it doesn't only take a dream, it takes also the will, the means, the plans, and a support network to accomplish it. Your mother's dreams to marry a David Schumerman had many obstacles including the limited-ness of choices, and a strong opposition on my part, to name just a few. However, those obstacles didn't deter you to go ahead with your plans to make your mother's dreams a reality. If it weren't because of your determination to make your mother's happy, and if it weren't because of the means you put into action to accomplish her dreams, today none of us could have been present in this room for this ceremony. [*She shakes Arketta's hand.*] Thank you again Arketta for relieving me from this bur-den. [*She points at David Sr.*] I really never loved David. He was a pin on my ass for all the time we lived together. He head dreams about marrying a rich woman. I guess his dream has become true today. [*Pause.*] Before all this happen we decided to break up and no longer live together. [*She pauses and look around.*] I believe now everybody got a piece of his coin. Arleta got David Schumerman to accomplish her dreams; my son, David Jr. got his Lynnette, the girl of his dreams; Arketta got the wedding for her mother; David Sr. got the rich woman of his dreams; and I got the money, a lot of money [*She waves the check*], and a rid of a man I hate the most. [*She points at David Sr.*] So, thank you everybody, and enjoy the rest of the ceremony.

Applauds from the attendees.

Curtain.

THE END

About the Author

D_____ R_____ Congo native Peddar Panga immigrated to the United States at thirty-years old. He graduated from Texas A&M University, San Antonio, with a bachelor's degree in biology and a minor in psychology. He majored in drama, nursing, and general science at San Antonio College.

Panga, who is multilingual, interprets for others as a hobby. He speaks English, French, Portuguese, Spanish, Swahili, and several other African languages. Along with writing, he loves travel, singing, acting, and sports. He volunteers at health care facilities and is a soccer referee.

www.ingramcontent.com/pod-product-compliance
Lightning Source LLC
Chambersburg PA
CBHW060942040426
42445CB00011B/966